Oh! MY SPEAKING 4

CEDU BOOK

UNIT COMPONENTS

KEY PATTERNS

Key words and key patterns are presented in context.
Students can role-play the conversation used in the cartoon.

VOCABULARY

Vocabulary words can be used immediately through activities related to pattern sentences.

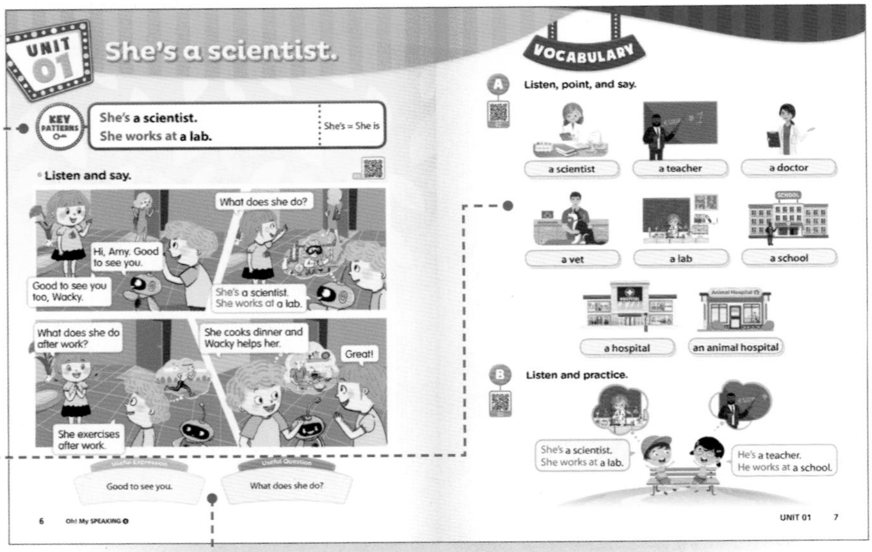

UNIT 01
She's a scientist.
KEY PATTERNS
She's a scientist.
She works at a lab.
She's = She is
Listen and say.
What does she do?
Hi, Amy. Good to see you.
Good to see you too, Wacky.
She's a scientist. She works at a lab.
What does she do after work?
She cooks dinner and Wacky helps her.
Great!
She exercises after work.
Useful Expression
Good to see you.
Useful Question
What does she do?
6 Oh! My SPEAKING
VOCABULARY
A Listen, point, and say.
a scientist
a teacher
a doctor
a vet
a lab
a school
a hospital
an animal hospital
B Listen and practice.
She's a scientist. She works at a lab.
He's a teacher. He works at a school.
UNIT 01 7

USEFUL EXPRESSIONS & QUESTIONS

A variety of particularly useful expressions from the dialogues in the cartoons allow students to develop their speaking skills.

KEY PATTERN PRACTICE

Repeating sentences with key patterns helps students to naturally remember what they have learned.

LISTEN AND SPEAK

Substituting words in key patterns in a combined listening and speaking activity assists students to build their speaking fluency.

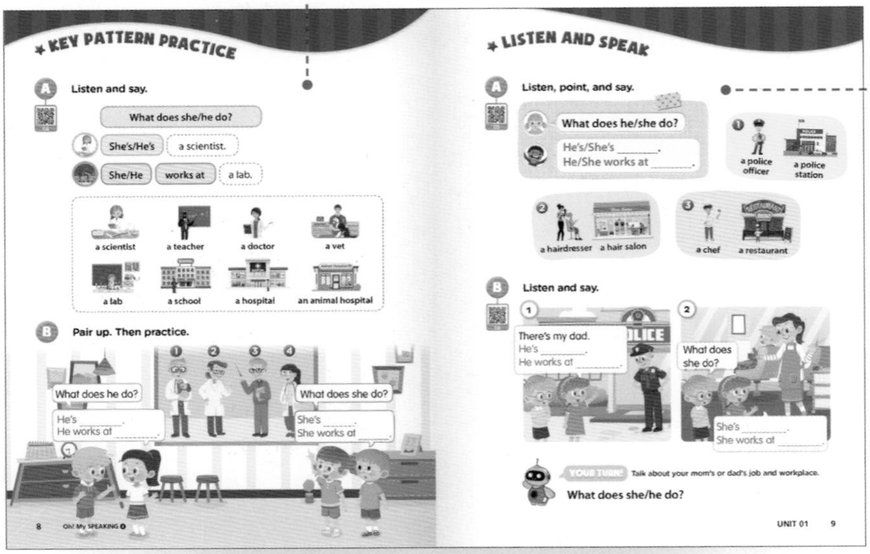

KEY PATTERN PRACTICE
A Listen and say.
What does she/he do?
She's/He's
a scientist.
She/He
works at
a lab.
a scientist
a teacher
a doctor
a vet
a lab
a school
a hospital
an animal hospital
B Pair up. Then practice.
What does he do?
He's ___. He works at ___.
What does she do?
She's ___. She works at ___.
8 Oh! My SPEAKING
LISTEN AND SPEAK
A Listen, point, and say.
What does he/she do?
He's/She's ___.
He/She works at ___.
a police officer
a police station
a hairdresser
a hair salon
a chef
a restaurant
B Listen and say.
There's my dad.
He's ___.
He works at ___.
What does she do?
She's ___.
She works at ___.
YOUR TURN! Talk about your mom's or dad's job and workplace.
What does she/he do?
UNIT 01 9

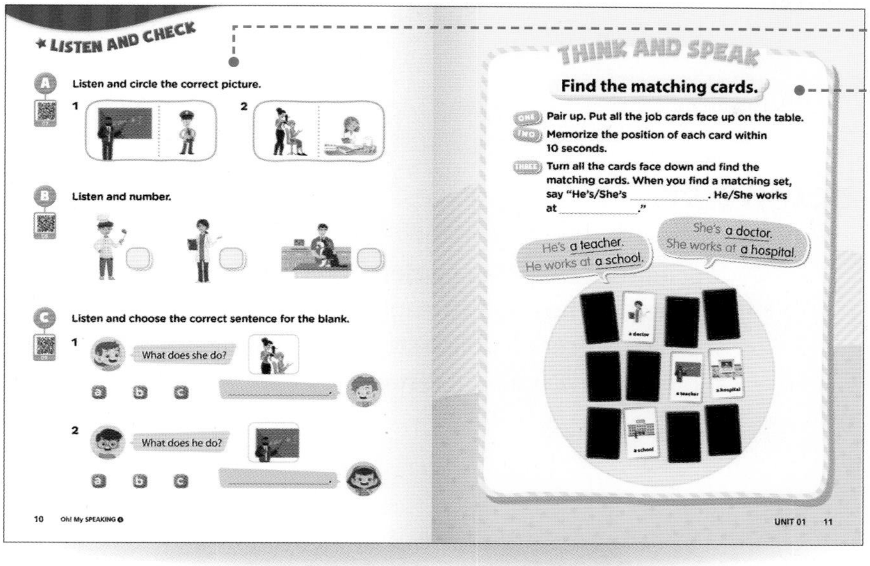
★ LISTEN AND CHECK

A Listen and circle the correct picture.

B Listen and number.

C Listen and choose the correct sentence for the blank.

1 What does she do? a b c

2 What does he do? a b c

10 Oh! My SPEAKING

THINK AND SPEAK

Find the matching cards.

ONE Pair up. Put all the job cards face up on the table.

TWO Memorize the position of each card within 10 seconds.

THREE Turn all the cards face down and find the matching cards. When you find a matching set, say "He's/She's ________. He/She works at ________."

He's a teacher. He works at a school.
She's a doctor. She works at a hospital.

UNIT 01 11

• LISTEN AND CHECK

Listening practice gets students to relate the key sentences to the pictures and to learn how to use the right sentences in the conversation.

• THINK AND SPEAK

A fun and educational communication game gets students to practice key sentences repeatedly.

REVIEW TEST

Word reviews and a variety of speaking and listening activities help students recall and further practice key words and key patterns from previous units.

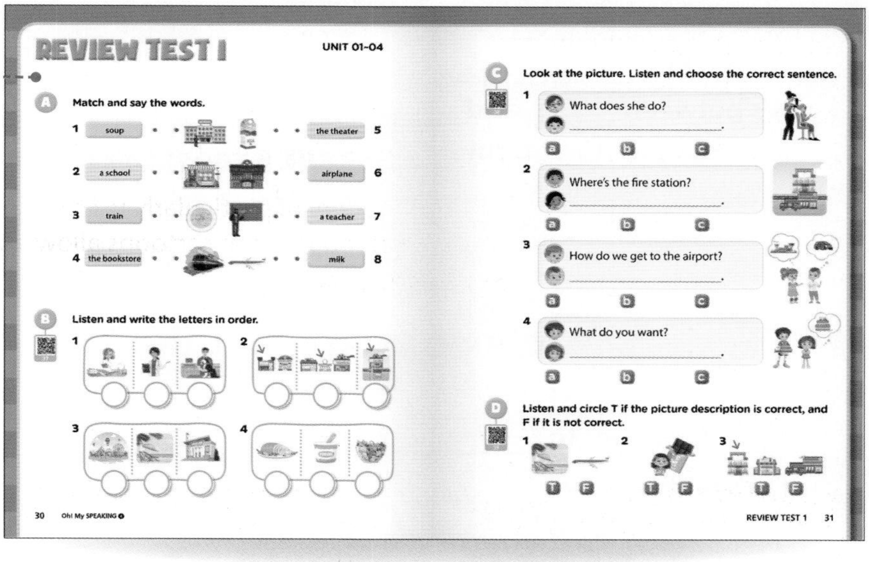
REVIEW TEST 1 UNIT 01-04

A Match and say the words.

1	soup	the theater	5
2	a school	airplane	6
3	train	a teacher	7
4	the bookstore	milk	8

B Listen and write the letters in order.

C Look at the picture. Listen and choose the correct sentence.

1 What does she do? a b c

2 Where's the fire station? a b c

3 How do we get to the airport? a b c

4 What do you want? a b c

D Listen and circle T if the picture description is correct, and F if it is not correct.

30 Oh! My SPEAKING — REVIEW TEST 1 31

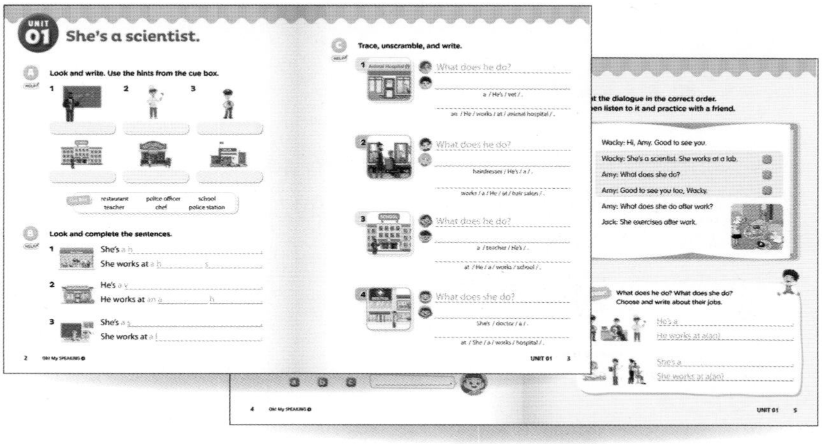
UNIT 01 She's a scientist.

A Look and write. Use the hints from the cue box.

Cue box: restaurant, police officer, school, teacher, chef, police station

B Look and complete the sentences.

1 She's a h______. She works at a h______.

2 He's a v______. He works at an a______ h______.

3 She's a s______. She works at a l______.

C Trace, unscramble, and write.

1 What does he do? a / He's / vet / . — an / He / works / at / animal hospital / .

2 What does he do? hairdresser / He's / a / . — works / a / He / at / hair salon / .

3 What does he do? a / teacher / He's / . — at / He / a / works / school / .

4 What does she do? She's / doctor / a / . — at / She / a / works / hospital / .

2 Oh! My SPEAKING — UNIT 01 3

...t the dialogue in the correct order. ...en listen to it and practice with a friend.

Wacky: Hi, Amy. Good to see you.

Wacky: She's a scientist. She works at a lab.

Amy: What does she do?

Amy: Good to see you too, Wacky.

Amy: What does she do after work?

Jack: She exercises after work.

What does he do? What does she do? Choose and write about their jobs.

He's a ______ He works at a(an) ______

She's a ______ She works at a(an) ______

4 Oh! My SPEAKING — UNIT 01 5

WORKBOOK

Various writing, listening, and speaking exercises allow students to review key words and key patterns learned in the Student Book.

CONTENTS

UNIT 01

She's a scientist.

KEY PATTERNS

She's a scientist.
She works at a lab.

She's = She is

01

Listen and say.

Hi, Amy. Good to see you.
Good to see you too, Wacky.
What does she do?
She's a scientist. She works at a lab.
What does she do after work?
She exercises after work.
She cooks dinner and Wacky helps her.
Great!

Useful Expression

Good to see you.

Useful Question

What does she do?

VOCABULARY

A Listen, point, and say.

02

a scientist

Lesson #1

a teacher

a doctor

a vet

a lab

SCHOOL

a school

HOSPITAL

a hospital

Animal Hospital
OPEN

an animal hospital

B Listen and practice.

03

She's a scientist.
She works at a lab.
He's a teacher.
He works at a school.

★ KEY PATTERN PRACTICE

A Listen and say.

04

What does she/he do?

She's/He's | a scientist.

She/He | **works at** | a lab.

a scientist

a teacher

a doctor

a vet

a lab

a school

a hospital

an animal hospital

B Pair up. Then practice.

1
2
3
4
What does he do?
He's ________.
He works at ________.
What does she do?
She's ______.
She works at ______.

LISTEN AND SPEAK

A Listen, point, and say.

05

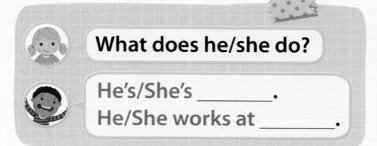

What does he/she do?

He's/She's ________.
He/She works at ________.

1

a police officer — a police station

2

a hairdresser — a hair salon

3

a chef — a restaurant

B Listen and say.

06

1

There's my dad.
He's ________.
He works at ________.

2

What does she do?
She's ________.
She works at ________.

YOUR TURN! Talk about your mom's or dad's job and workplace.

What does she/he do?

★ LISTEN AND CHECK

A Listen and circle the correct picture.

07

1 
Lesson #1

2 

B Listen and number.

08

 ☐

 ☐

 ☐

C Listen and choose the correct sentence for the blank.

09

1 

What does she do?

a b c

______________________.

2 

What does he do?

Lesson #1

a b c

______________________.

THINK AND SPEAK

Find the matching cards.

ONE Pair up. Put all the job cards face up on the table.

TWO Memorize the position of each card within 10 seconds.

THREE Turn all the cards face down and find the matching cards. When you find a matching set, say "He's/She's ______________. He/She works at ______________."

He's a teacher.
He works at a school.

She's a doctor.
She works at a hospital.

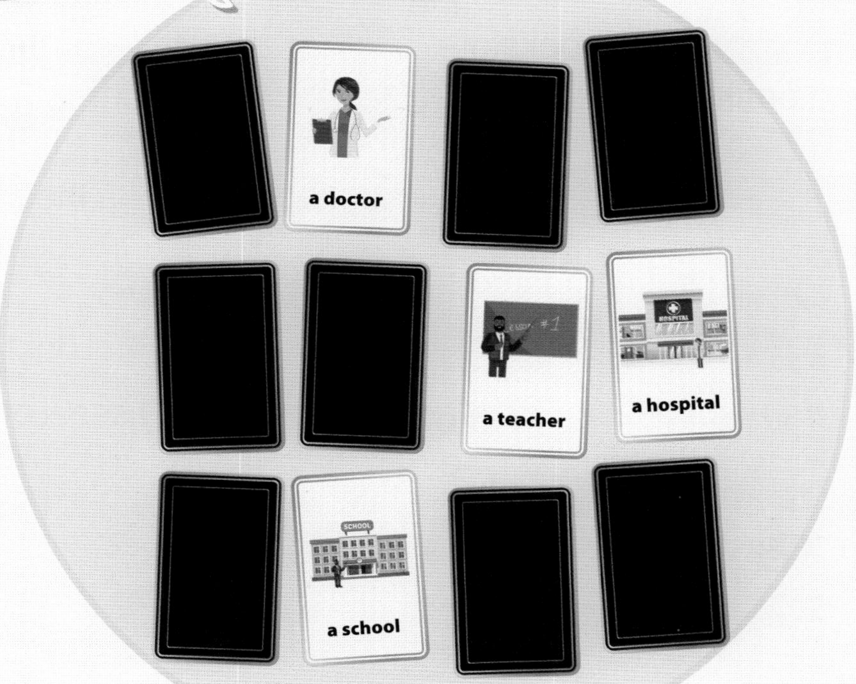

a doctor
a teacher
a hospital
a school

UNIT 02 Where's the bookstore?

KEY PATTERNS

Where's **the bookstore**?
It's next to **the bank.**

Where's = Where is
It's = It is

Listen and say.

10

Let's go to the bookstore.
Where's the bookstore?
It's next to the bank.
Where's the bank?
It's behind the donut shop.
Where's the donut shop?
It's between the theater and the stationery store.
Where's the theater?
It's across the street from the bus stop. Look!
Oh, I see. Let's go.
BUS STOP

Useful Expression

Let's go to the bookstore.

Useful Question

Where's the bank?

VOCABULARY

A Listen, point, and say.

11

the bookstore
the bank
Donut!
THEATER
the stationery store
the donut shop
the theater
BUS
the bus stop

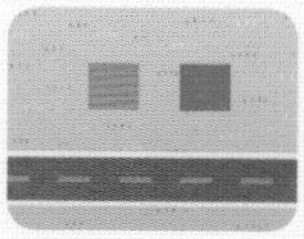

next to

between A and B

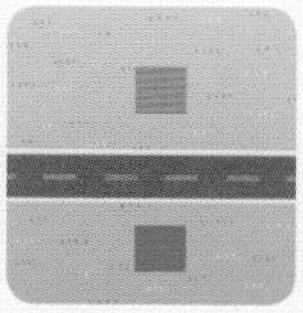

across the street from

B Listen and practice.

12

Where's the bookstore?
It's next to the bank.

★ KEY PATTERN PRACTICE

A Listen and say.

13

Where's | the bookstore?

It's | next to | the bank.

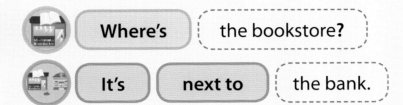

the bookstore
the bank
the stationery store
the donut shop
Donut!
THEATER
the theater
BUS
the bus stop

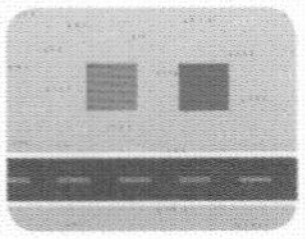

next to

across the street from

between A and B

B Pair up. Then practice.

1
2
3
4
Donut!
THEATER
Where's ______?
It's ______.

★ LISTEN AND SPEAK

A Listen, point, and say.

14

Where's ___________?

It's ___________.

1 the bakery
2 the park
PARK
3 the library
4 the playground
5 the market
6 the fire station

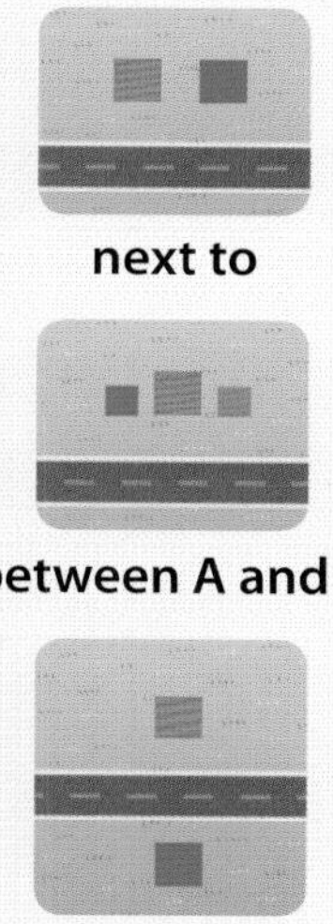

next to

between A and B

across the street from

B Listen and say.

15

1

Where's the bakery?
PARK
It's ___________.

2

Where's the market?
It's ___________.

YOUR TURN! Ask and answer about the places around your town.

Where's the bookstore?

★ LISTEN AND CHECK

A Listen and choose the correct sentence.

16

1

ⓐ ⓑ

2

BUS

ⓐ ⓑ

3

Donut!
THEATER

ⓐ ⓑ

B Listen and number.

17

THEATER
BUS
PARK

C Listen and choose the correct sentence for the blank.

18

1

ⓐ ⓑ ⓒ

Where's the fire station?

__________________________.

2

BUS
Donut!

ⓐ ⓑ ⓒ

__________________________?

It's between the bus stop and the donut shop.

THINK AND SPEAK

My Town

Draw and look at your town. Then take turns asking and answering with your friend.

Where's the theater?

It's across the street from the bakery.

UNIT 03 Let's go there by bike.

KEY PATTERNS

How do we get to the amusement park?
Let's go there by bike.

Let's = Let us

19

- **Listen and say.**

How do we get to the amusement park?
Let's see.
Let's go there by bike.
No. It's too far. Let's go there by bus.
Do you see this? There are so many cars.
Oh no!
Let's go there by subway.
Good idea!

Useful Expressions

Let's see. / It's too far.
Good idea!

Useful Question

Do you see this?

VOCABULARY

A Listen, point, and say.

20

the amusement park

the beach

bike

bus

car

subway

train

TAXI

taxi

B Listen and practice.

21

How do we get to the amusement park?
Let's go there by bike.

★ KEY PATTERN PRACTICE

A Listen and say.

22

 How | do we | get to | the amusement park?

 Let's | go | there | **by** bike.

the amusement park

the beach

bike

bus

car

subway

train

taxi

B Pair up. Then practice.

1
2
3
4
BUS
TAXI
How do we get to the amusement park?
Let's go there by ___________.

★ LISTEN AND SPEAK

A Listen, point, and say.

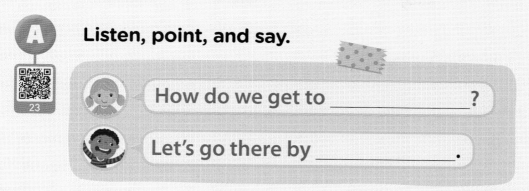

23

How do we get to ________________?

Let's go there by ________________.

AIRPORT

the airport

MUSEUM

the museum

1 airplane

2 ship

3 boat

B Listen and say.

24

1

MUSEUM
How do we get to ________________?
Let's go there by ________________.

2

AIRPORT
How do we get to ________________?
Let's go there by ________________.

YOUR TURN! Talk about the form of transportation you will use.

How do we get to the beach?

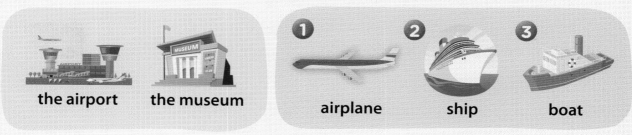

★ LISTEN AND CHECK

A Listen and circle the correct picture.

25

1 
TAXI

2 

B Listen and number.

26

MUSEUM

C Listen and check T for True or F for False.

27

1 Jack, Wacky, and Mom will go to the amusement park.

T ☐ F ☐

2 The amusement park is far from them.

T ☐ F ☐

3 Jack, Wacky, and Mom will go there by bike.

T ☐ F ☐

THINK AND SPEAK

How do we get there?

ONE **Pair up. Take turns and roll a die.**
Ask and answer according to the number.

How do we get to ________ ? (place)

Let's go there by ________ . (transportation)

Place

1 the lab
2 the bookstore
3 the donut shop
4 the theater
5 the amusement park
6 the beach

Transportation

1 bike
2 bus
3 taxi
4 subway
5 airplane
6 train

TWO **Student A: Flip one 'Reaction Card' and say it.**

THREE **Student B: Say your own opinion.**

How do we get to the theater?

Let's go there by bike.

Oh no! It's too far!

Reaction Card
"Oh no! It's too far!"

Let's go there by bus.

UNIT 04 I want some ice cream.

KEY PATTERNS

I want some **ice cream.**
I don't want any **ice cream.**

don't = do not

Listen and say.

28

What do you want?
I want some ice cream.
Do you want some ice cream, too?
No. I don't want any ice cream.
Hamburger
I just want some water. Do you want some water, too?
No. I don't want any water.
Oh no! My ice cream!
Wow! I want some ice cream juice!

Useful Expression

Oh no!

Useful Questions

What do you want?
Do you want some ice cream?

VOCABULARY

A Listen, point, and say.

29

Choco

chocolate

Bubble Gum

gum

POPCORN

popcorn

ham

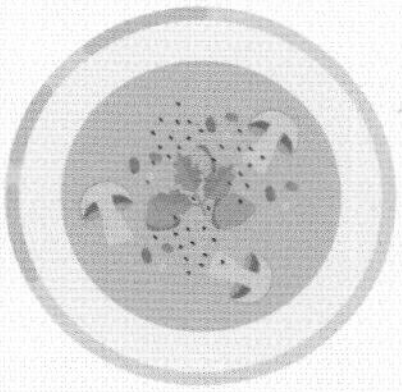

soup

juice

water

MILK

milk

B Listen and practice.

30

I want some chocolate.
I don't want any chocolate.

★ KEY PATTERN PRACTICE

A Listen and say.

31

Do you want some chocolate?

Yes.	I	want	some	chocolate.
No.	I	don't	want	any	chocolate.

chocolate
gum
popcorn
ham
soup
juice
water
milk

B Pair up. Then practice.

What do you want?
I want some ____________.
Do you want some ____________?
No. I don't want any ____________.

LISTEN AND SPEAK

A Listen, point, and say.

32

Do you want some ____?

Yes. I want some ____________.

No. I don't want any ____________.

1 
butter

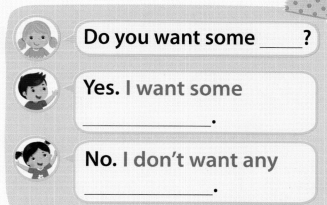

2 
salad

3 
bacon

4 
YOGURT
yogurt

5 
sausage

6 
cake

B Listen and say.

33

1

What do you want?
Yogurt
MENU
Yogurt
I want some ____________.

2

Do you want some ____________?
No. I don't want any ____________.

YOUR TURN! Talk about the kind of food you want and don't want.

What food do you want?

★ LISTEN AND CHECK

A Listen and choose the correct sentence.

34

1 
MILK

a b

2 

a b

3 
POPCORN

a b

B Listen and draw O below the food if the child wants it.

35

YOGURT

C Listen and check T for True or F for False.

36

1 Jack wants some ice cream.

T ☐ F ☐

2 Amy wants some ice cream.

T ☐ F ☐

3 Amy just wants some water.

T ☐ F ☐

THINK AND SPEAK

At the Supermarket

ONE **Look at the grocery list and check what you want.**

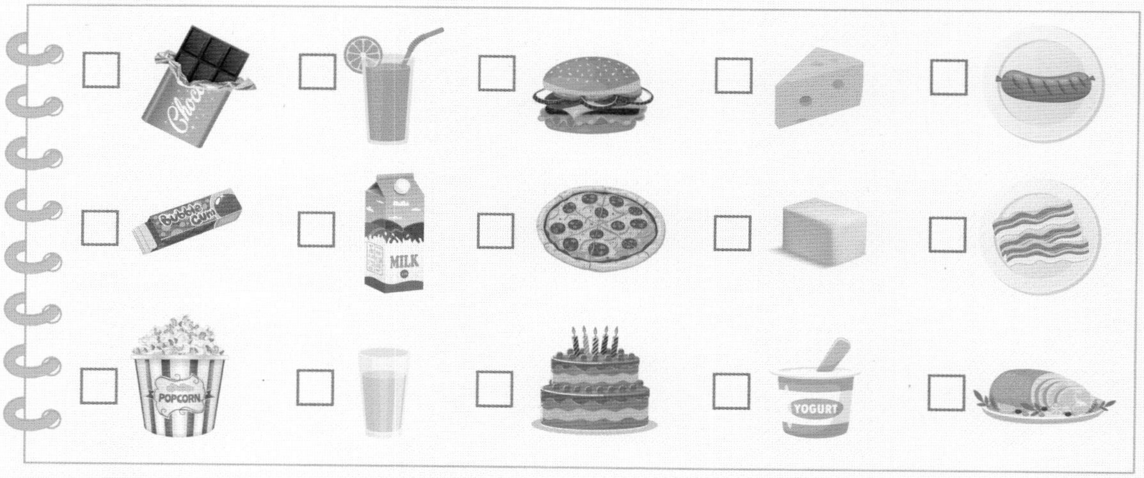
MILK
POPCORN
YOGURT

TWO **Pair up and role-play as below.**

What do you want?
I want some pizza.
Do you want some pizza, too?
No. I don't want any pizza.
I want some cake.
-%
G SALE
SPECIAL OFFER
SUPER PRICE
MILK
FRUITS
VEGETABLES
MEAT
SEAFOOD

REVIEW TEST I

UNIT 01~04

A Match and say the words.

1	soup			the theater	5
2	a school			airplane	6
3	train	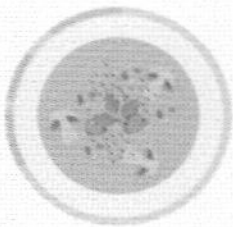		a teacher	7
4	the bookstore			milk	8

SCHOOL
MILK
BOOKS
THEATER

B Listen and write the letters in order.

37

1 

2 

THEATER
THEATER

3 

MUSEUM

4 

YOGURT

C Look at the picture. Listen and choose the correct sentence.

38

1

What does she do?

______________________________.

a b c

2

Where's the fire station?

______________________________.

a b c

3

How do we get to the airport?

______________________________.

a b c

4

What do you want?

______________________________.

a b c

D Listen and circle T if the picture description is correct, and F if it is not correct.

39

1

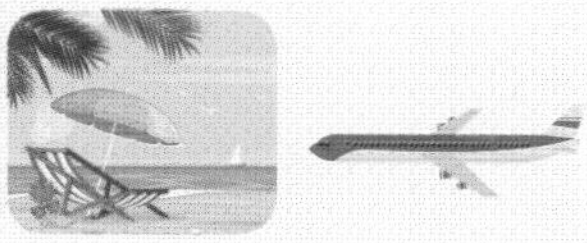

T F

2

T F

3

T F

REVIEW TEST 1

E Talk about your town.

STEP 1 Choose and write the correct words for each blank.

across the street from the theater **taxi** **next to the donut shop** **the bookstore**

Let's go to ________________.

Where's the bookstore?

It's ________________.

Where's the donut shop?

It's ________________ ________________.

How do we get there?

It's too far. Let's go there by ________________.

Great idea!

Donut!
THEATER

STEP 2 Where's the bookstore? Draw a map of your imaginary town.

STEP 3 How do we get there? Write and talk about it with your friends.

Let's go to ____________________.
(place)

It's ______________________________.
(location)

It's ______________________________.
(location)

Let's go there by ____________________.
(transportation)

UNIT 05

I was in the bedroom.

KEY PATTERNS

I was in **the bedroom.**
I wasn't in **the living room.**

wasn't = was not

Listen and say.

40

What a mess! Were you in the living room, Jack?
No. I wasn't in the living room.
Where were you all day?
I was at my friend's house.
Where was Lily this morning?
I don't know. I was in the bedroom all day.
Where was she?
I remember! She was in the living room!

Useful Expressions

What a mess!
I remember!

Useful Questions

Were you in the living room?
Where were you all day?

VOCABULARY

A Listen, point, and say.

41

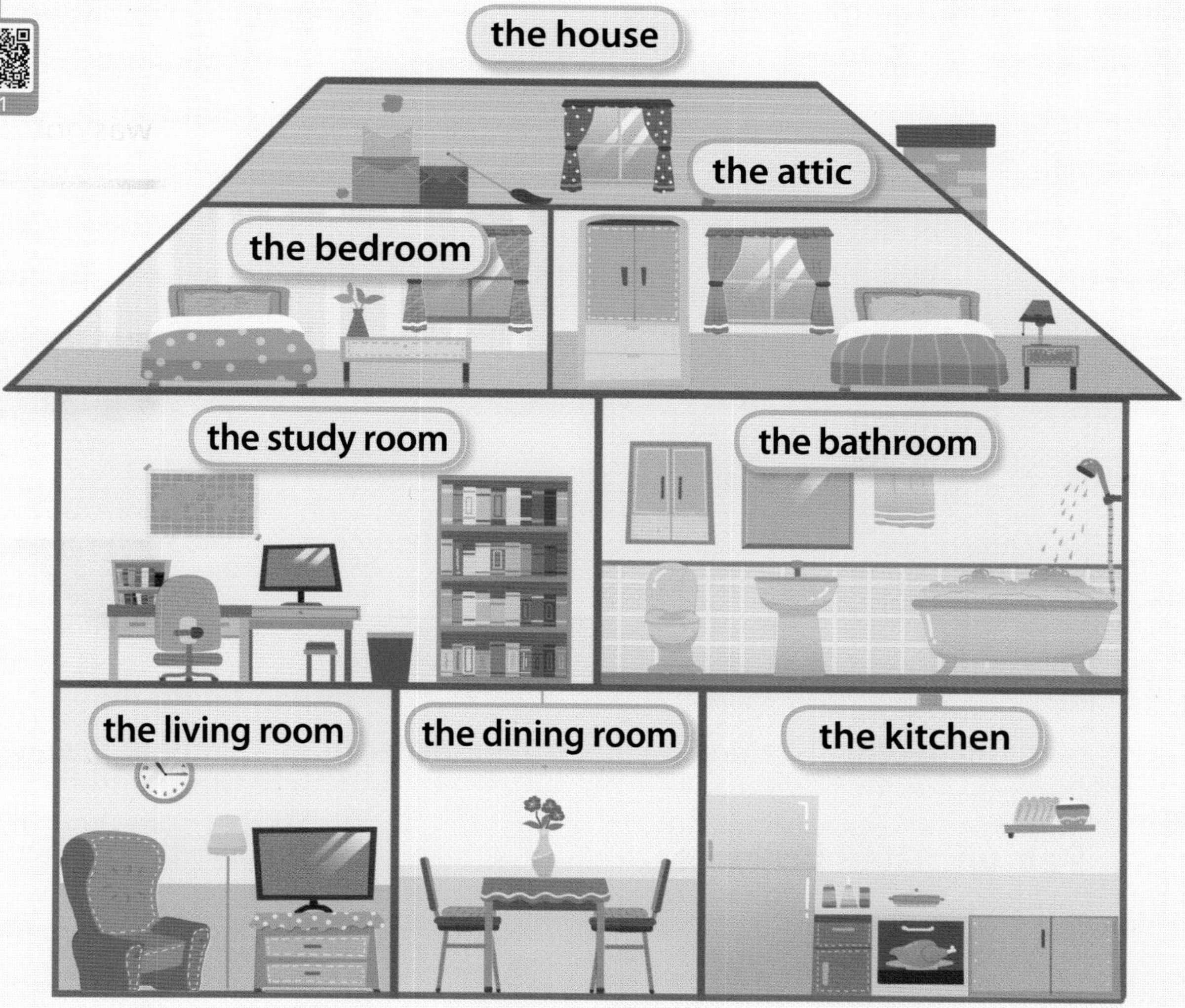
the house
the attic
the bedroom
the study room
the bathroom
the living room
the dining room
the kitchen

B Listen and practice.

42

I was in the house.
I wasn't in the house.

★ KEY PATTERN PRACTICE

A Listen and say.

43

Were you in the house?

 Yes. | I | was | in | the house.

 No. | I | wasn't | in | the house.

the house

the attic

the bedroom

the study room

the bathroom

the living room

the dining room

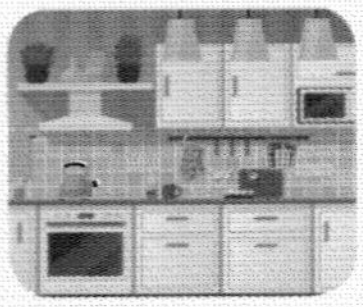
the kitchen

B Pair up. Then practice.

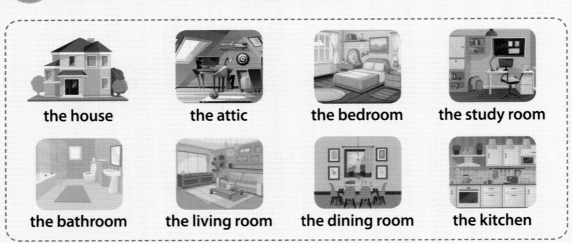

1
2
3
4
Where were you?
Were you in ________?
Yes. I was in ________.
No. I wasn't in ________.

★ LISTEN AND SPEAK

A Listen, point, and say.

44

Were you in ______?

Yes. I was in ______.

No. I wasn't in ______.

1 the garage
2 the garden
3 the backyard

B Speak about yourself.

Where were you?

1 I was in ______________________.

2 I was in ______________________.

3 I was in ______________________.

YOUR TURN! Talk about the places you were at.

Where were you?

★ LISTEN AND CHECK

A Listen and choose the correct sentence.

45

1 

ⓐ ⓑ

2 

ⓐ ⓑ

3 

ⓐ ⓑ

B Listen and number.

46

C Listen and choose the correct sentence for the blank.

47

1 

ⓐ ⓑ ⓒ

Where were you all day?

______________________________.

2 

ⓐ ⓑ ⓒ

Were you in the garden?

______________________________.

THINK AND SPEAK

Where were you?

ONE **Look at the picture. Draw people in different parts of the house.**

Ken

Mom

Dad

Lily

TWO **Pair up and role-play as below.**

Where were you all day, Ken?

I was in the study room. Where were you all day, Mom?

I was in the living room.

UNIT 06

I was nervous.

KEY PATTERNS

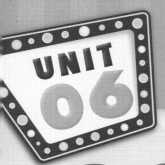

I was **nervous.**
I wasn't **bored.**

wasn't = was not

Listen and say.

48

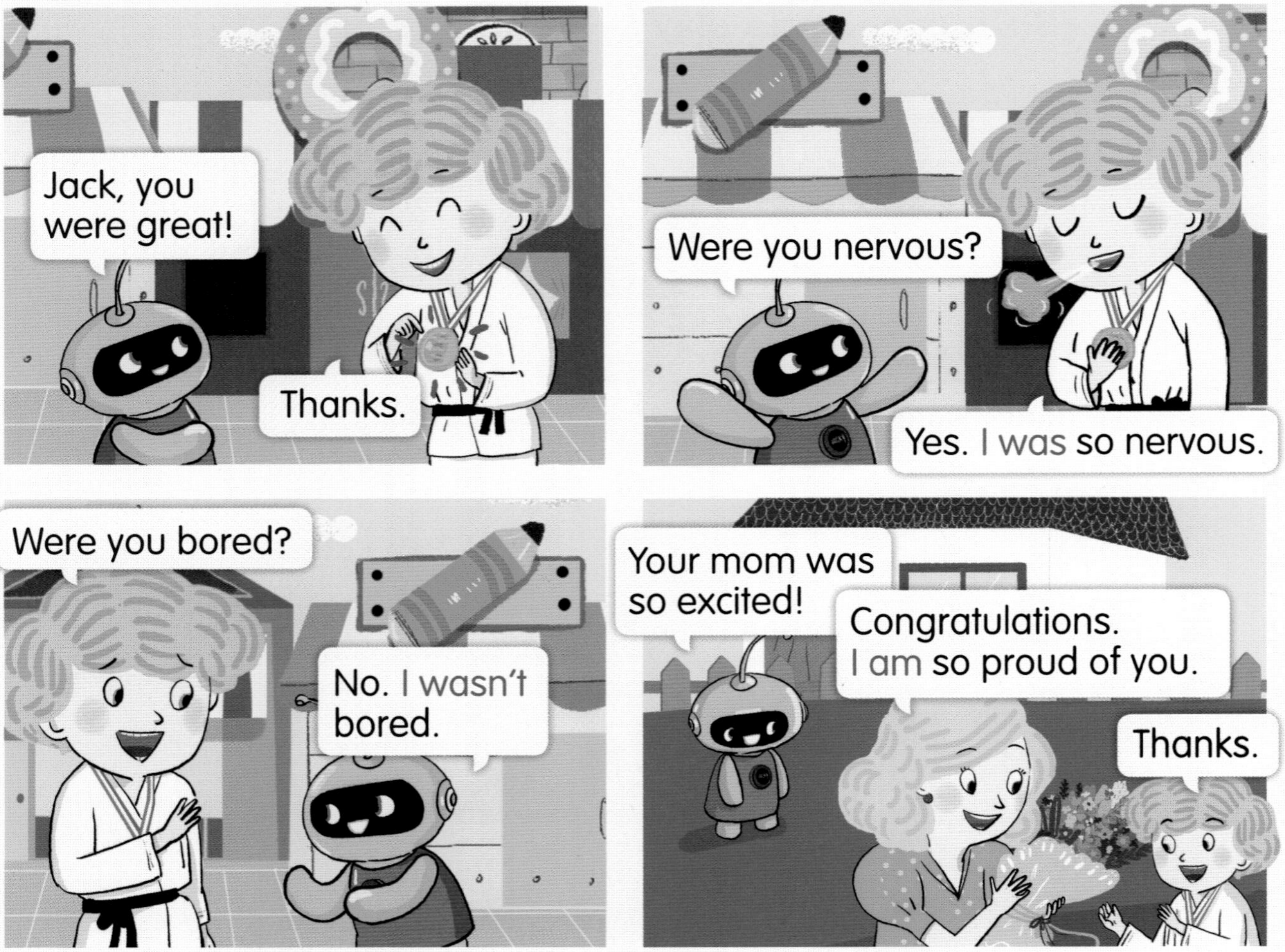
Jack, you were great!
Thanks.
Were you nervous?
Yes. I was so nervous.
Were you bored?
No. I wasn't bored.
Your mom was so excited!
Congratulations. I am so proud of you.
Thanks.

Useful Expressions

Congratulations.
I am so proud of you.

Useful Question

Were you nervous?

VOCABULARY

A Listen, point, and say.

49

HAUNTED
HOUSE

nervous

sleepy

bored

glad

brave

calm

surprised

worried

upset

B Listen and practice.

50

I was nervous.
I wasn't nervous.

★ KEY PATTERN PRACTICE

A Listen and say.

51

Were you nervous?

Yes.	I	was	nervous.
No.	I	wasn't	nervous.

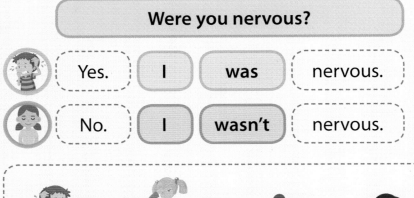

nervous

sleepy

bored

glad

brave

calm

surprised

worried

upset

B Pair up. Then practice.

1
2
Were you ________?
Yes. I was ________.
3
4
Were you ________?
No. I wasn't upset. I was calm.
No. I wasn't calm. I was upset.

★ LISTEN AND SPEAK

A Listen, point, and say.

52

Were you ____________?

Yes. I was ____________.

No. I wasn't ____________.

1 
unhappy

2 
amazed

3 
tired

4 
curious

5 
satisfied

6 
stressed

B Listen and say.

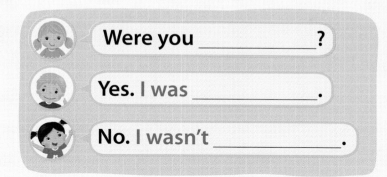

53

1 
Were you a__________?
Yes. I was __________.

2 
Were you satisfied?
No. I wasn't __________.

YOUR TURN! Ask and answer about your friend's situation in the past.

Were you nervous?

★ LISTEN AND CHECK

A Listen and choose the correct sentence.

54

1 

ⓐ ⓑ

2 

ⓐ ⓑ

3 

ⓐ ⓑ

B Listen and number.

55

 ☐

 ☐

 ☐

C Listen and choose the correct sentence for the blank.

56

1 

Were you stressed?

a b c

______________________.

2 

Were you nervous?

a b c

______________________.

THINK AND SPEAK

How did you feel?

ONE Pair up.

TWO Roll the die and play the game.

Feeling Flashcard Don't show or tell the word to your partner. Mime the word and have your partner guess the answer until he/she gets it right.

Situation Card Read the situation card out loud. Express your own feeling that best fits the situation.

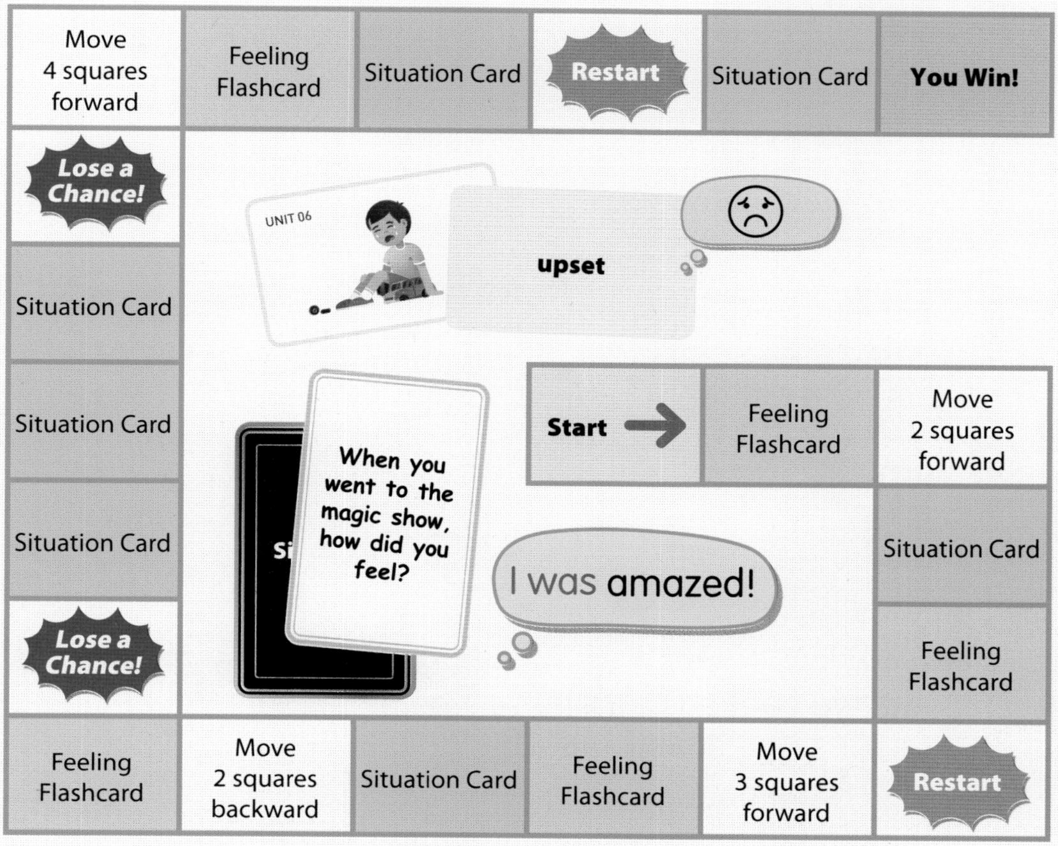
Start
Feeling Flashcard
Move 2 squares forward
Situation Card
Feeling Flashcard
Restart
Move 3 squares forward
Feeling Flashcard
Situation Card
Move 2 squares backward
Feeling Flashcard
Lose a Chance!
Situation Card
Situation Card
Situation Card
Lose a Chance!
Move 4 squares forward
Feeling Flashcard
Situation Card
Restart
Situation Card
You Win!
UNIT 06
upset
When you went to the magic show, how did you feel?
I was amazed!

UNIT 07

I played football.

KEY PATTERNS

I played football.
I didn't practice the piano.

didn't = did not

57

Listen and say.

What did you do today?
I played football and studied math.
Did you practice the piano?
No. I didn't practice the piano.
What?
Sorry.
But we cooked dinner!
That's okay. You cooked dinner. Thank you.
You're welcome.

Useful Expression

That's okay.

Useful Questions

What did you do today?
Did you practice the piano?

VOCABULARY

A Listen, point, and say.

58

practiced the piano

played football

studied math

cooked dinner

baked cookies

watched TV

painted a picture

brushed the dog

practice → practiced
play → played
study → studied
cook → cooked
bake → baked
watch → watched
paint → painted
brush → brushed

B Listen and practice.

59

I practice every day.

I practiced yesterday.

I didn't practice yesterday.

★ KEY PATTERN PRACTICE

A Listen and say.

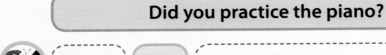

Did you practice the piano?

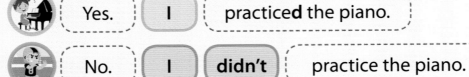

Yes. | I | practice**d** the piano.

No. | I | **didn't** | practice the piano.

practiced the piano

played football

studied math

cooked dinner

baked cookies

watched TV

painted a picture

brushed the dog

B Pair up. Then practice.

Did you ________?
Yes. I ________.
1
2
3
4
No. I didn't
________.

★ LISTEN AND SPEAK

A Listen, point, and say.

61

Did you ________?

Yes. I ________.

No. I didn't ________.

1 
listened to music

2 
played chess

3 
walked the dog

4 
cleaned the room

5 
patted a cat

6 
washed the car

listen → listened
play → played
walk → walked
clean → cleaned
pat → patted
wash → washed

B Speak about yourself.

What did you do?

1 I ________________.

2 I ________________.

3 I ________________.

YOUR TURN! Talk about what you did in the past.

What did you do yesterday?

★ LISTEN AND CHECK

A Listen and circle the correct picture.

62

1

2

B Listen and number.

63

 ☐

 ☐

 ☐

C Listen and choose the correct sentence for the blank.

64

1

Did you clean the room?

a b c ______________________. 

2

What did you do today?

a b c ______________________. 

THINK AND SPEAK

Role-play

ONE **Check what you did last weekend.**

TWO **Pair up. Fill in the blanks and role-play with your partner.**

You: I ________ then ________ today.

What did you do?

Friend: I ________ .

You: What else? Did you study math?

Friend: No. I didn't study math. I ________

then I ________ in the living room.

UNIT 08 I had fun.

KEY PATTERNS

I had fun.
I didn't have fun.

didn't = did not

65

Listen and say.

What did you do?
I went to a baseball game with Wacky.
Did you have fun?
Yes. I had fun! I saw famous players!
No. I didn't have fun.
What did you eat?
I ate a hot dog. Mmm, so good!
I didn't eat anything.
I made some cookies.
Yummy! Thanks!

Useful Expression

So good!

Useful Question

Did you have fun?

VOCABULARY

A Listen, point, and say.

66

went to a baseball game

saw famous players

HOT DOG

ate a hot dog

SODA

drank soda

made cookies

read a book

rode a bike

had fun

go → went
see → saw
eat → ate
drink → drank
make → made
read → read
ride → rode
have → had

B Listen and practice.

67

I went to a baseball game.

I didn't go to a baseball game.

★ KEY PATTERN PRACTICE

A Listen and say.

68

What did you do?

I | went | to a baseball game.

I | didn't | go | to a baseball game.

went to
a baseball game

saw
famous players

HOT DOG

ate a hot dog

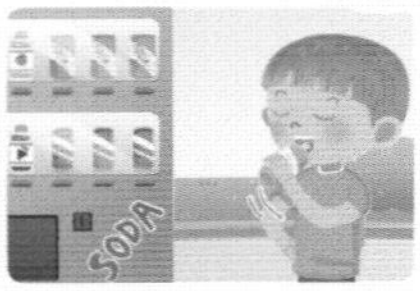
SODA

drank soda

made cookies

read a book

rode a bike

had fun

B Pair up. Then practice.

What did you do?
I ________.
I didn't ________.
1
2
I ________.
3
4
I didn't ________.

★ LISTEN AND SPEAK

A Listen, point, and say.

69

What did you do?

I ________.

I didn't ________.

1 
sang a song

2 
ran a mile

3 
did my homework

4 
took a bath

5 
fed my dog

6 
flew a kite

sing → sang
run → ran
do → did
take → took
feed → fed
fly → flew

B Listen and say.

70

1 
What did you do?
I ________.

2 
What did you do?
I ________, but I didn't ________.

YOUR TURN! With your friends, talk about what you did last weekend.

What did you do last weekend?

★ LISTEN AND CHECK

A Listen and choose the correct sentence.

71

1 
SODA

a b

2 

a b

3 

a b

B Listen and number.

72

 ☐

 ☐

 ☐

C Listen and check T for True or F for False.

73

1 Jack went to a baseball game.

T ☐ F ☐

2 Jack didn't see any famous players.

T ☐ F ☐

3 Jack didn't eat anything.

T ☐ F ☐

THINK AND SPEAK

What did you do?

ONE Fill in the blanks with the past tense of the words in the word box.

make	fly	read	go	take

TWO Write your own story in the blanks for Thursday and Saturday.

THREE Pair up. Ask questions and provide answers based on the sentences below.

What did you do on Monday?

I made cookies.

Last Week's Schedule

Monday
I made cookies.

Tuesday
I ______ a book.

Wednesday
I ______ a kite.

Thursday
______
______
______.

Friday
I ______ a bath.

Saturday
______
______
______.

Sunday
I ______ to a baseball game.

REVIEW TEST 2

UNIT 05~08

A Match and say the words.

1 surprised

2 sleepy

3 the bedroom

4 the bathroom

5 cleaned the room

6 sang a song

7 took a bath

8 watched TV

B Listen and write the letters in order.

74

1

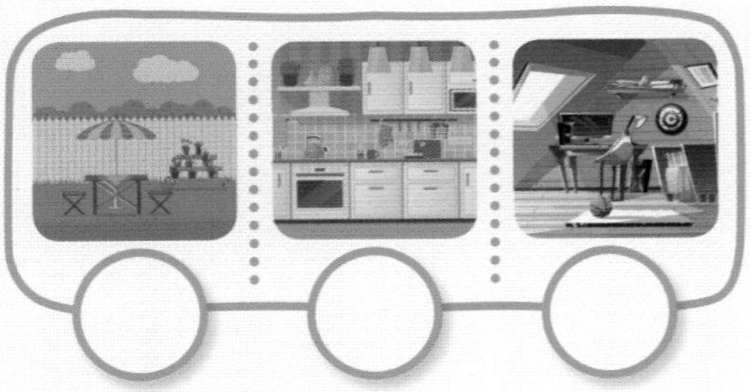

2

3

4

SODA

C Look at the picture. Listen and choose the correct sentence.

75

1 Were you in the kitchen?

______________________________.

a b c

2 Were you curious?

______________________________.

a b c

3 What did you do?

______________________________.

a b c

4 What did you do?
Did you see famous players?

______________________________.

a b c

D Listen and circle T if the picture description is correct, and F if it is not correct.

76

1

T F

2

T F

3

T F

E Talk about your day.

STEP 1 Choose and write the correct words for each blank.

did my homework | I didn't see | I went | I was in the study room | I had fun

Where were you?

________________________________.

What did you do?

I ______________________________.
Then ______________________
to a baseball game
with my dad.

Did you see famous players?

No. ________________ famous players, but ____________!

Great!

STEP 2 Draw a circle around the things you did yesterday.

HOT DOG
SODA

STEP 3 What did you do yesterday? Write and talk about it with your friends.

I was in ____________________ *yesterday.*
(place)

I ____________________.
(activity)

Then I ____________________.
(activity)

I didn't ____________________,
(activity)

but I ____________________.
(activity)

SCOPE & SEQUENCE

UNIT 01 She's a scientist.

Key Patterns	Vocabulary	Useful Expression	Goals
She's **a scientist.** She works at **a lab.**	a scientist / a teacher / a doctor / a vet / a lab / a school / a hospital / an animal hospital / a police officer / a police station / a hairdresser / a hair salon / a chef / a restaurant	Good to see you. **Useful Question** What does she do?	• Talking about jobs • Talking about workplaces Theme Jobs / Workplaces

UNIT 02 Where's the bookstore?

Key Patterns	Vocabulary	Useful Expression	Goals
Where's **the bookstore**? It's next to **the bank.**	the bookstore / the bank / the stationery store / the donut shop / the theater / the bus stop / next to / between A and B / across the street from / the bakery / the park / the library / the playground / the market / the fire station	Let's go to the bookstore. **Useful Question** Where's the bank?	• Talking about places • Talking about locations Theme Places

UNIT 03 Let's go there by bike.

Key Patterns	Vocabulary	Useful Expressions	Goals
How do we get to **the amusement park**? Let's go there by **bike.**	the amusement park / the beach / bike / bus / car / subway / train / taxi / the airport / the museum / airplane / ship / boat	Let's see. It's too far. Good idea! **Useful Question** Do you see this?	• Talking about places and transportation • Making suggestion Theme Mode of transportation

UNIT 04 I want some ice cream.

Key Patterns	Vocabulary	Useful Expression	Goals
I want some **ice cream.** I don't want any **ice cream.**	chocolate / gum / popcorn / ham / soup / juice / water / milk / butter / salad / bacon / yogurt / sausage / cake	Oh no! **Useful Questions** What do you want? Do you want some ice cream?	• Talking about desires • Making affirmative/negative statements Theme What you want to eat

REVIEW TEST 1 UNIT 01-04

UNIT 05 I was in the bedroom.

Key Patterns	Vocabulary	Useful Expressions	Goals
I was in **the bedroom.** I wasn't in **the living room.**	the house / the attic / the bedroom / the study room / the bathroom / the living room / the dining room / the kitchen / the garage / the garden / the backyard	What a mess! I remember! **Useful Questions** Were you in the living room? Where were you all day?	• Talking about the rooms in the house • Using the verb "to be" in the past tense • Making affirmative/negative statements Theme Places in the house

UNIT 06 I was nervous.

Key Patterns	Vocabulary	Useful Expressions	Goals
I was **nervous.** I wasn't **bored.**	nervous / sleepy / bored / glad / brave / calm / surprised / worried / upset / unhappy / amazed / tired / curious / satisfied / stressed	Congratulations. I was so proud of you. **Useful Question** Were you nervous?	• Asking in past tense • Talking about feelings and states • Making affirmative/negative statements Theme Feelings

UNIT 07 I played football.

Key Patterns	Vocabulary	Useful Expression	Goals
I **play**ed **football.** I didn't **practice the piano.**	practiced the piano / played football / studied math / cooked dinner / baked cookies / watched TV / painted a picture / brushed the dog / listened to music / played chess / walked the dog / cleaned the room / patted a cat / washed the car	That's okay. **Useful Questions** What did you do today? Did you practice the piano?	• Talking about past events • Using regular past tense verbs • Making affirmative/negative statements Theme My day

UNIT 08 I had fun.

Key Patterns	Vocabulary	Useful Expression	Goals
I had **fun.** I didn't have **fun.**	went to a baseball game / saw famous players / ate a hot dog / drank soda / made cookies / read a book / rode a bike / had fun / sang a song / ran a mile / did my homework / took a bath / fed my dog / flew a kite	So good! **Useful Question** Did you have fun?	• Talking about past events • Using irregular verbs • Making affirmative/negative statements Theme Free time

REVIEW TEST 2 UNIT 05-08

WORD LIST

a scientist

Lesson #1

a teacher

a doctor

a lab

SCHOOL

a school

HOSPITAL

a hospital

a vet

Animal Hospital
OPEN

an animal hospital

a police officer

a hairdresser

a chef

POLICE
POLICE

a police station

Hair Salon

a hair salon

RESTAURANT
BISTRO

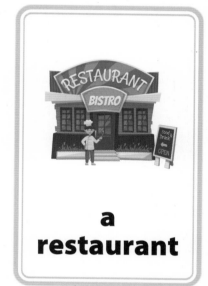

a restaurant

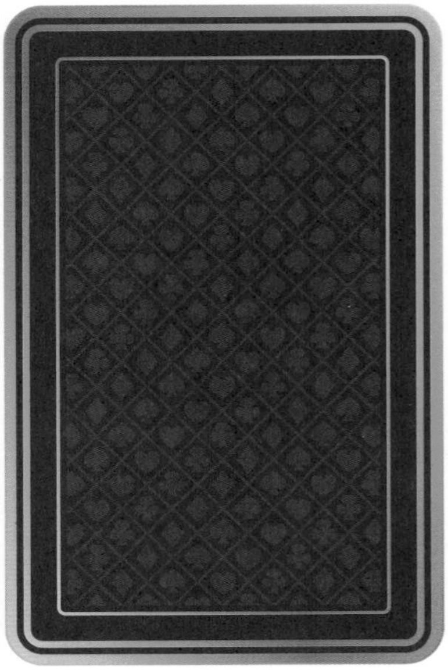

 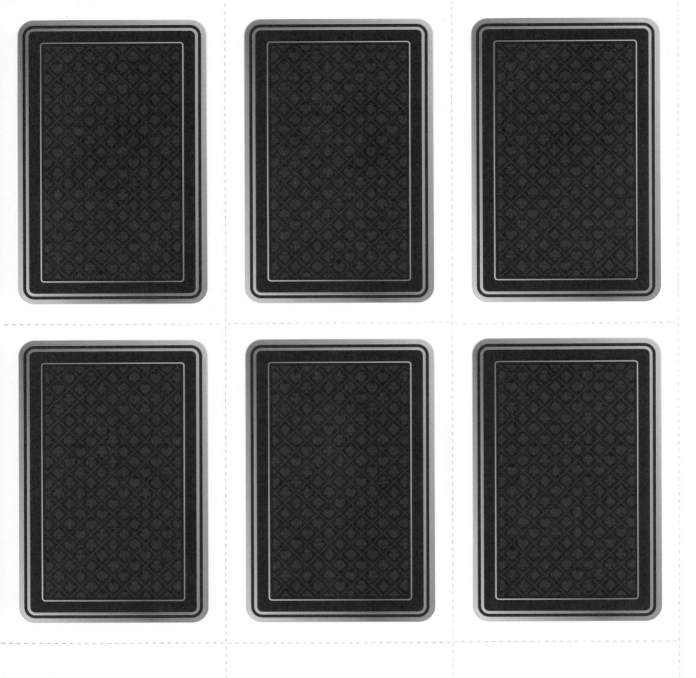

"Oh no!
It's
too far!"

"Oh!
It's close."

"Oh,
I'm late.
Let's hurry."

"There are
so many
cars."

"There are
so many
people."

Reaction
Card

Reaction
Card

Reaction
Card

Reaction
Card

Reaction
Card

When you lost the game, how did you feel?

When you went to an amusement park, how did you feel?

When you went to the magic show, how did you feel?

When you got a present, how did you feel?

When you lost your bag, how did you feel?

When you watched a long documentary movie, how did you feel?

When you took an exam, how did you feel?

Situation Card

Situation Card

Situation Card

Situation Card

Situation Card

Situation Card

Situation Card

UNIT 01

UNIT 01

Lesson #1

UNIT 01

UNIT 01

UNIT 01

UNIT 01

SCHOOL

UNIT 01

HOSPITAL

UNIT 01

Animal Hospital
OPEN

UNIT 01

UNIT 01

POLICE
POLICE

UNIT 01

UNIT 01

Hair Salon

UNIT 01

UNIT 01

RESTAURANT
BISTRO
OPEN

UNIT 02

UNIT 02

$

VOCABULARY FLASHCARDS

a vet	**a doctor**	**a teacher**	**a scientist**
an animal hospital	**a hospital**	**a school**	**a lab**
a hair salon	**a hairdresser**	**a police station**	**a police officer**
the bank	**the bookstore**	**a restaurant**	**a chef**

UNIT 02

UNIT 02

Donut!

UNIT 02

THEATER

UNIT 02

BUS

UNIT 02

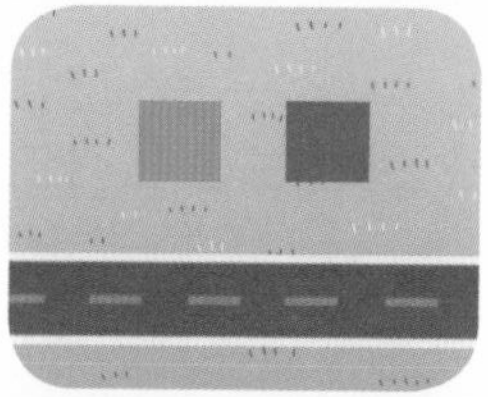

UNIT 02

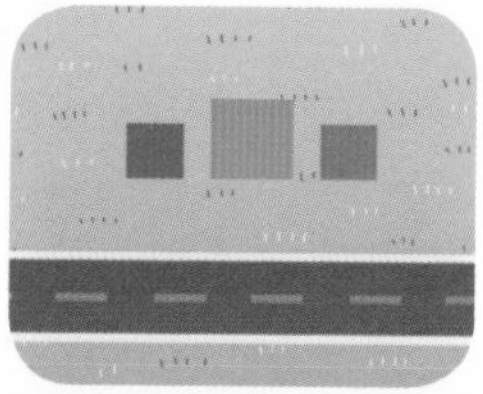

UNIT 02

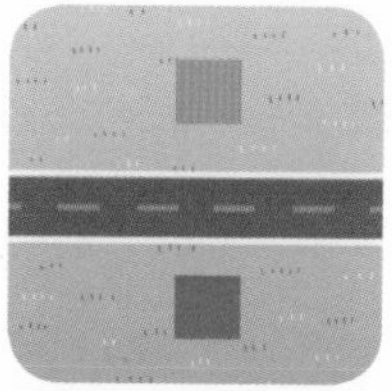

UNIT 02

UNIT 02

UNIT 02

UNIT 02

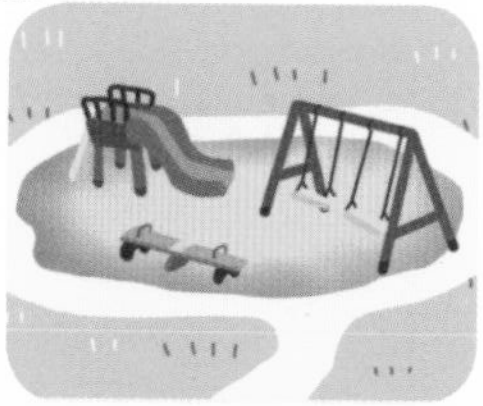

UNIT 02

UNIT 02

UNIT 03

UNIT 03

UNIT 03

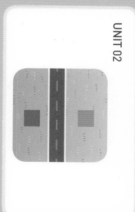

VOCABULARY FLASHCARDS

the bus stop	the theater	the donut shop	the stationery store
the bakery	across the street from	between A and B	next to
the market	the playground	the library	the park
bike	the beach	the amusement park	the fire station

VOCABULARY FLASHCARDS

UNIT 03

UNIT 03

UNIT 03

UNIT 03

UNIT 03

TAXI

UNIT 03

AIRPORT

UNIT 03

MUSEUM

UNIT 03

UNIT 03

UNIT 03

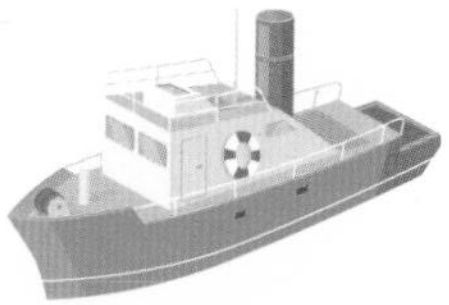

UNIT 04

UNIT 04

Bubble
Gum

UNIT 04

POPCORN

UNIT 04

UNIT 04

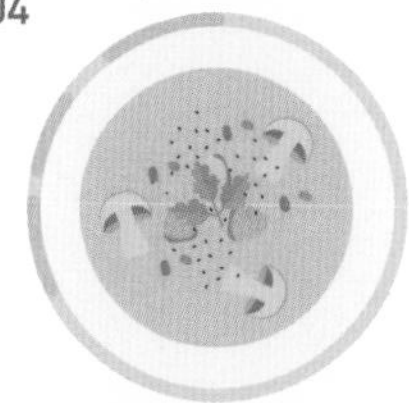

UNIT 04

train	**subway**	**car**	**bus**
airplane	**the museum**	**the airport**	**taxi**
gum	**chocolate**	**boat**	**ship**
juice	**soup**	**ham**	**popcorn**

UNIT 04

UNIT 04

MILK

UNIT 04

UNIT 04

UNIT 04

UNIT 04

YOGURT

UNIT 04

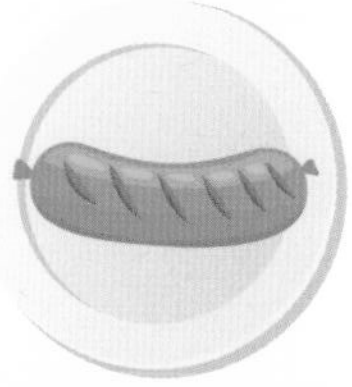

UNIT 04

UNIT 05

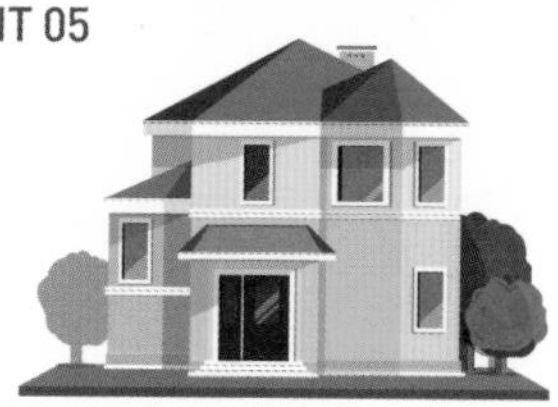

UNIT 05

UNIT 05

UNIT 05

UNIT 05

UNIT 05

UNIT 05

UNIT 05

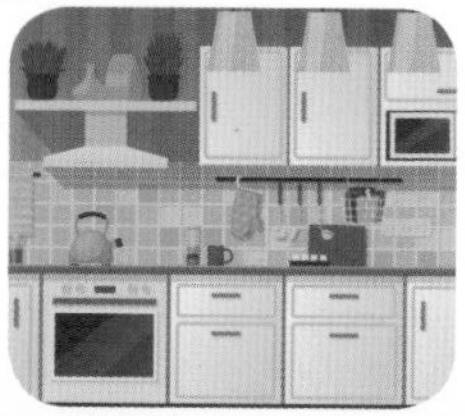

VOCABULARY FLASHCARDS

salad	**butter**	**milk**	**water**
cake	**sausage**	**yogurt**	**bacon**
the study room	**the bedroom**	**the attic**	**the house**
the kitchen	**the dining room**	**the living room**	**the bathroom**

UNIT 05

UNIT 05

UNIT 05

UNIT 06

HAUNTED
HOUSE

UNIT 06

UNIT 06

UNIT 06

UNIT 06

UNIT 06

UNIT 06

UNIT 06

UNIT 06

UNIT 06

UNIT 06

UNIT 06

UNIT 06

VOCABULARY FLASHCARDS

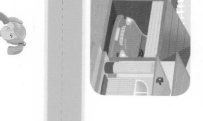

nervous	**the backyard**	**the garden**	**the garage**
brave	**glad**	**bored**	**sleepy**
upset	**worried**	**surprised**	**calm**
curious	**tired**	**amazed**	**unhappy**

UNIT 06

UNIT 06

UNIT 07

practice the piano

UNIT 07

play football

UNIT 07

study math

UNIT 07

cook dinner

UNIT 07

bake cookies

UNIT 07

watch TV

UNIT 07

paint a picture

UNIT 07

brush the dog

UNIT 07

listen to music

UNIT 07

play chess

UNIT 07

walk the dog

UNIT 07

clean the room

UNIT 07

pat a cat

UNIT 07

wash the car

VOCABULARY FLASHCARDS

played football	**practiced the piano**	**stressed**	**satisfied**
watched TV	**baked cookies**	**cooked dinner**	**studied math**
played chess	**listened to music**	**brushed the dog**	**painted a picture**
washed the car	**patted a cat**	**cleaned the room**	**walked the dog**

UNIT 08

go to a baseball game

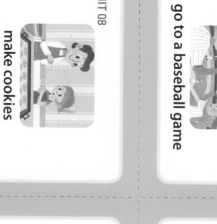

UNIT 08

see famous players

UNIT 08

HOT DOG

eat a hot dog

UNIT 08

SODA

drink soda

UNIT 08

make cookies

UNIT 08

read a book

UNIT 08

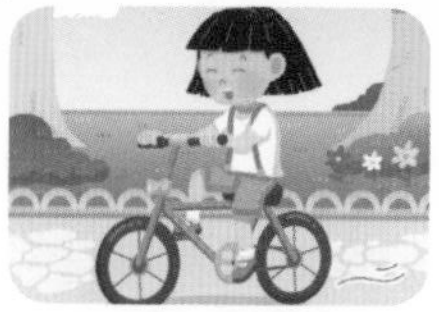

ride a bike

UNIT 08

have fun

UNIT 08

sing a song

UNIT 08

run a mile

UNIT 08

do my homework

UNIT 08

take a bath

UNIT 08

feed my dog

UNIT 08

fly a kite

VOCABULARY FLASHCARDS

drank soda	ate a hot dog	saw famous players	went to a baseball game
had fun	rode a bike	read a book	made cookies
took a bath	did my homework	ran a mile	sang a song
		flew a kite	fed my dog

UNIT 01

She's

UNIT 01

He's

UNIT 01

She works at

UNIT 01

He works at

UNIT 02

Where's

UNIT 02

It's next to

UNIT 02

It's between ___ and ___.

UNIT 02

It's across the street from

PATTERN FLASHCARDS

UNIT 03

How do we get to

UNIT 03

Let's go there by

UNIT 04

I want some

UNIT 04

I don't want any

UNIT 05

I was in

UNIT 05

I wasn't in

UNIT 06

I was

UNIT 06

I wasn't

PATTERN FLASHCARDS

UNIT 07

I

UNIT 07

I didn’t

UNIT 08

I

UNIT 08

I didn’t

.

.

?

?

PATTERN FLASHCARDS

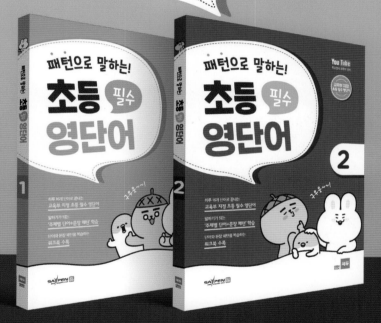

쎄듀런

1 구문 판매 1위 '천일문' 콘텐츠를 활용하여 정확하고 다양한 구문 학습

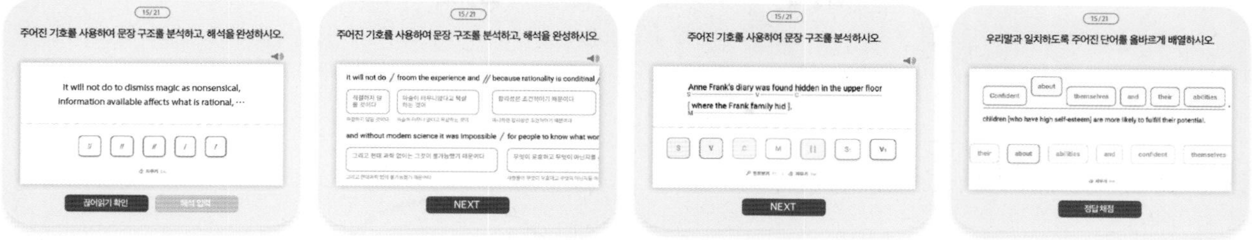

끊어읽기 | 해석하기 | 문장 구조 분석 | 해설·해석 제공 | 단어 스크램블링 | 영작하기

2 문법·서술형 쎄듀의 모든 문법 문항을 활용하여 내신까지 해결하는 정교한 문법 유형 제공

객관식과 주관식의 결합 | 문법 포인트별 학습 | 보기를 활용한 집합 문항 | 내신대비 서술형 | 어법+서술형 문제

3 어휘 초·중·고·공무원까지 방대한 어휘량을 제공하며 오프라인 TEST 인쇄도 가능

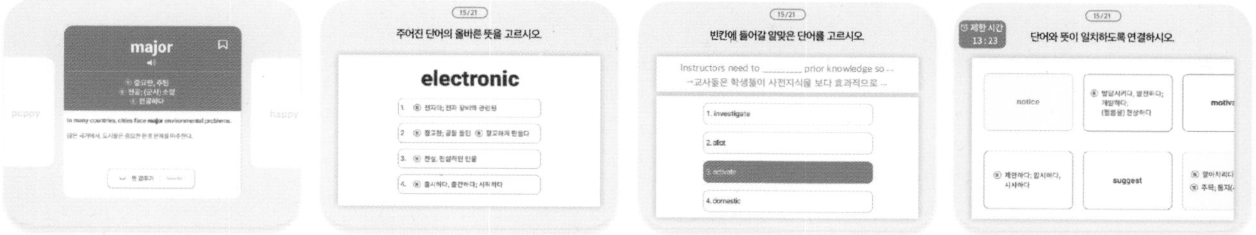

영단어 카드 학습 | 단어 ↔ 뜻 유형 | 예문 활용 유형 | 단어 매칭 게임

4 선생님 보유 문항 이용

Online Test | OMR Test

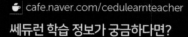

cafe.naver.com/cedulearnteacher

쎄듀런 학습 정보가 궁금하다면?

쎄듀런 Cafe

- 쎄듀런 사용법 안내 & 학습법 공유
- 공지 및 문의사항 QA
- 할인 쿠폰 증정 등 이벤트 진행

Oh! MY SPEAKING

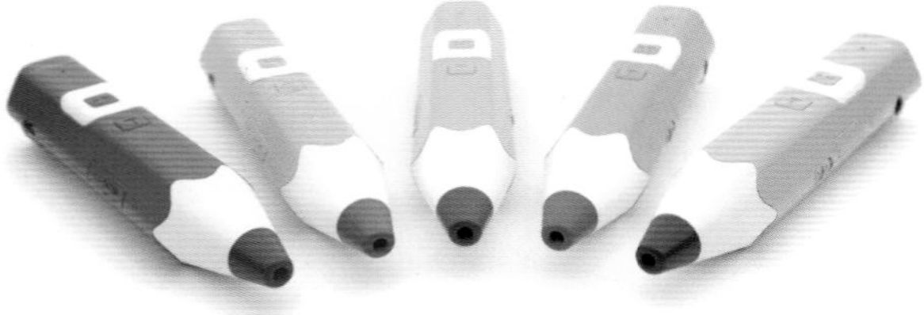

with 세이펜 SAYPEN TV

원어민 음성을 실시간 반복학습	단어 및 대화의 우리말 해석 듣기	선생님의 Workbook Guide로 혼자서도 쉽게 학습

세이펜 핀파일 다운로드 안내

STEP 1 세이펜과 컴퓨터를 USB 케이블로 연결하세요.

STEP 2 쎄듀북 홈페이지(www.cedubook.com)에 접속 후, 학습자료실 메뉴에서 학습할 교재를 찾아 이동합니다.

> 초등교재 ▶ ELT ▶ 학습교재 클릭 ▶ 세이펜 핀파일 자료 클릭
> ▶ 다운로드 (저장을 '다른 이름으로 저장'으로 변경하여 저장소를 USB로 변경) ▶ 완료

STEP 3 음원 다운로드가 완료되면 세이펜과 컴퓨터의 USB 케이블을 분리하세요.

STEP 4 세이펜을 분리하면 "시스템을 초기화 중입니다. 잠시만 기다려 주세요." 라는 멘트가 나옵니다.

STEP 5 멘트 종료 후 세이펜을 〈Oh! My Speaking〉 표지에 대보세요.
효과음이 나온 후 바로 학습을 시작할 수 있습니다.

참고사항

- 세이펜은 본 교재에 포함되어 있지 않습니다. 별도로 구매하여 이용할 수 있으며, 기존에 보유하신 세이펜이 있다면 핀파일만 다운로드해서 바로 이용하실 수 있습니다.
- 세이펜에서 제작된 모든 기종(기존에 보유하고 계신 기종도 호환 가능)으로 사용이 가능합니다.
- 모든 기종은 세이펜에서 권장하는 최신 펌웨어 업데이트를 진행해 주시기 바랍니다.
  업데이트는 세이펜 홈페이지(www.saypen.com)에서 가능합니다.
- 핀파일은 쎄듀북 홈페이지(www.cedubook.com)와 세이펜 홈페이지(www.saypen.com)에서 모두 다운로드 가능합니다.
- 세이펜을 이용하지 않는 학습자는 쎄듀북 홈페이지 부가학습자료, 교재 내 QR코드 이미지 등을 활용하여 원어민 음성으로 학습하실 수 있습니다.
- 기타 문의사항은 www.cedubook.com / 02-3272-4766으로 연락 바랍니다.

WORKBOOK

Oh! MY SPEAKING

4

with SAYPEN

MP3 CD Included

SAYPEN TV
www.saypen.com

CEDUBOOK

Oh! MY SPEAKING 4

WORKBOOK

CEDUBOOK

UNIT 01 She's a scientist.

A Look and write. Use the hints from the cue box.

HELP

1

Lesson #1

2

3

SCHOOL

RESTAURANT
BISTRO

POLICE

Cue Box			
	restaurant	police officer	school
	teacher	chef	police station

B Look and complete the sentences.

HELP

1

Hair Salon

She's a h____________________.

She works at a h__________ s__________.

2

Animal Hospital

He's a v____________________.

He works at an a__________ h__________.

3

She's a s____________________.

She works at a l____________________.

C Trace, unscramble, and write.

HELP

1

Animal Hospital
OPEN

What does he do?

____

a / He's / vet / .

____

an / He / works / at / animal hospital / .

2

What does he do?

____

hairdresser / He's / a / .

____

works / a / He / at / hair salon / .

3

SCHOOL

What does he do?

____

a / teacher / He's / .

____

at / He / a / works / school / .

4

HOSPITAL

What does she do?

____

She's / doctor / a / .

____

at / She / a / works / hospital / .

D What do they do? Listen and number.

77

HELP

Lesson #1

E Listen and choose the right sentence for the blank.

78

HELP

1

What does he do?

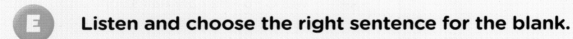

POLICE
POLICE

a b c

_______________________________.

2

What does she do?

a b c

_______________________________.

F

Put the dialogue in the correct order.
Then listen to it and practice with a friend.

79

HELP

Wacky: Hi, Amy. Good to see you.

Wacky: She's a scientist. She works at a lab. ☐

Amy: What does she do? ☐

Amy: Good to see you too, Wacky. ☐

Amy: What does she do after work?

Jack: She exercises after work.

YOUR TURN! What does he do? What does she do?
Choose and write about their jobs.

He's a ______________________.

He works at a(an) ______________________.

She's a ______________________.

She works at a(an) ______________________.

UNIT 02

Where's the bookstore?

A Write and find the words.

HELP

1 

______

2 

______

3 

______

4 

______

5 
THEATER

______

6 

______

b	i	t	h	e	a	t	e	r	q
o	i	z	a	w	c	l	o	w	l
o	t	a	o	b	i	u	r	j	i
k	n	t	j	a	q	u	t	s	b
s	w	r	s	n	b	n	z	a	r
t	y	t	a	k	r	g	c	d	a
o	g	q	d	r	a	f	k	e	r
r	k	m	a	r	k	e	t	a	y
e	q	s	t	a	o	r	g	x	r
w	c	x	b	a	k	e	r	y	v

B Look and complete the sentences.

HELP

1 

A: Where's the bank?

B: It's next to the b______.

2 
THEATER
BUS

A: Where's the theater?

B: It's across the street from the b______ s______.

3 
THEATER

A: Where's the donut shop?

B: It's between the s______ s______ and the t______.

C Trace, unscramble, and write.

HELP

1

BUS

Where's the market?

____

and the bus stop / It's / the bank / between / .

2

Where's the bookstore?

____

the stationery store / It's / next to / .

3

BUS

Where's the bank?

____

between / It's / and the donut shop / the bus stop / .

4

Where's the fire station?

____

It's / from the library / across / the street / .

D Where is it? Listen and number.

80

HELP

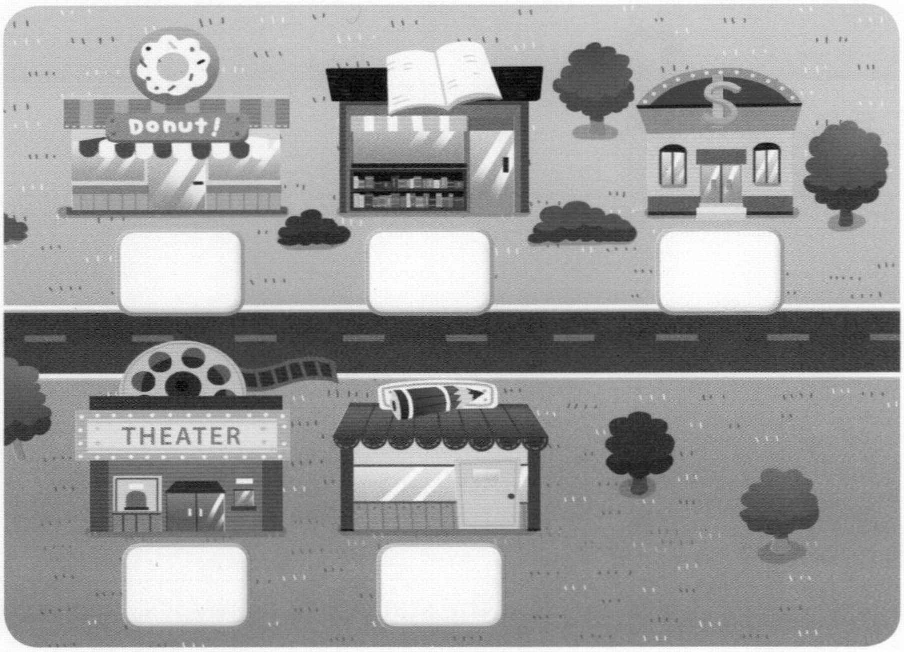

Donut!
THEATER

E Listen and choose the right sentence for the blank.

81

HELP

1

ⓐ ⓑ ⓒ

_______________________?

It's between the library and the fire station.

2

Donut!
THEATER

ⓐ ⓑ ⓒ

Where's the donut shop?

_______________________.

F

82

HELP

Put the dialogue in the correct order.
Then listen to it and practice with a friend.

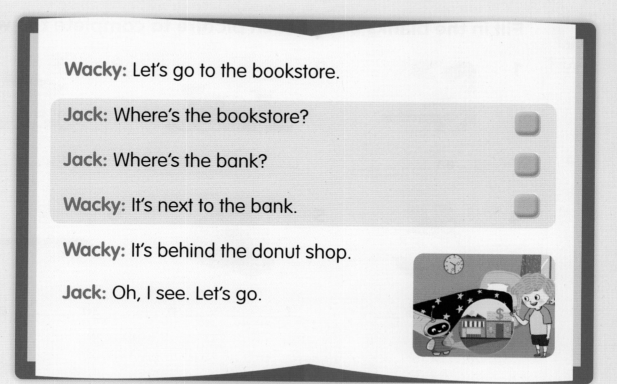

Wacky: Let's go to the bookstore.

Jack: Where's the bookstore? ☐

Jack: Where's the bank? ☐

Wacky: It's next to the bank. ☐

Wacky: It's behind the donut shop.

Jack: Oh, I see. Let's go.

YOUR TURN! Look at the map. Give the right direction.

A: Where's the playground?

B: It's ______________________.

A: Where's the fire station?

B: It's ______________________.

UNIT 03 Let's go there by bike.

A Fill in the blanks below each picture to complete the word.

HELP

1 

___ ea ___ ___

2 

___ ir ___ ___ rt

3 

___ u ___ e ___ ___

4 

___ ___ i ___

5 

t ___ ___ ___ n

6 

air ___ ___ a ___ e

B Look and complete the sentences.

HELP

1  

A: How do we get to the a ___________ p ___________?

B: Let's go there by t ___________.

2  

A: How do we get to the m ___________?

B: Let's go there by s ___________.

3  

A: How do we get to the b ___________?

B: Let's go there by b ___________.

C Trace, unscramble, and write.

HELP

1

How do we get to the museum?

____

by subway / there / Let's / go /.

2

____

get / How / we / do / to the beach / ?

Let's go there by airplane.

3

How do we get to the airport?

____

there / Let's / by car / go /.

4

____

we / do / to the amusement park / get / How / ?

Let's go there by train.

D How do we get there? Listen and number.

83

HELP

How do we get to the amusement park?

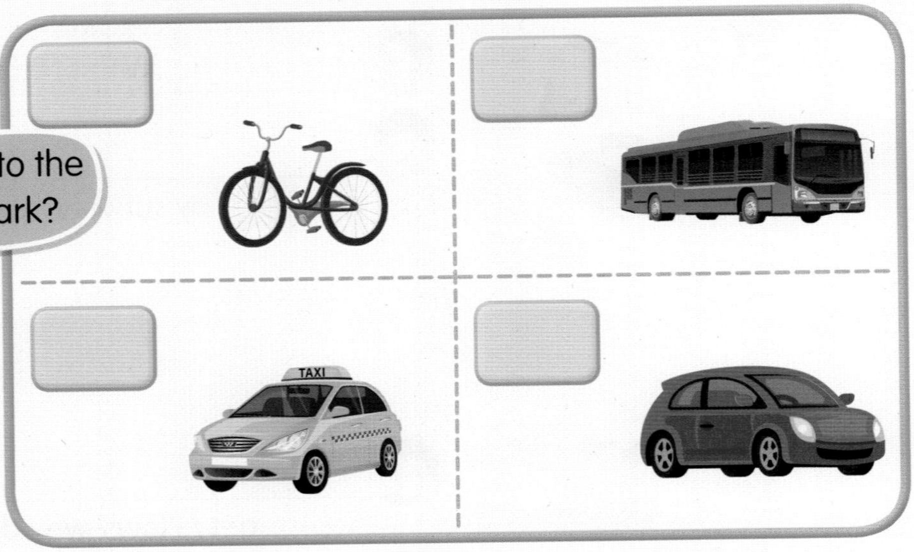
TAXI

E Listen and choose the right sentence for the blank.

84

HELP

1

AIRPORT

_______________?

Let's go there by car.

a b c

2

MUSEUM

How do we get to the museum?

_______________.

a b c

F

Put the dialogue in the correct order.
Then listen to it and practice with a friend.

85

HELP

Jack: How do we get to the amusement park?

Mom: No. It's too far. Let's go there by bus. ☐

Jack: Let's go there by bike. ☐

Wacky: Do you see this? There are so many cars. ☐

Wacky: Let's go there by subway.

Mom: Good idea!

YOUR TURN! How do we get to the amusement park?
Choose and write the form of transportation.

A: How do we get to the amusement park?

B: Let's go there by ______________________.

UNIT 04 I want some ice cream.

A Unscramble and write the words.

HELP

1

POPCORN

p c p
o r n o

____

2

YOGURT

r y o
t g u

____

3

a e w
r t

____

4

c n b
o a

____

5

i j c
u e

____

6

d s l
a a

____

B Look and complete the sentences.

HELP

1

POPCORN

I want some s__________.

I don't want any p__________.

2

MILK

I want some m__________.

I don't want any j__________.

3

I want some c__________.

I don't want any g__________.

C Trace, unscramble, and write.

HELP

1

What do you want?

some / want / I / ham / .

2

Do you want some ?

Yes.

I / cake / want / some / .

3

What do you want?

yogurt / I / some / want / .

4

Do you want some ?

No.

want / don't / salad / I / any / .

D Listen and draw O and X below the pictures.

86

HELP

1

2

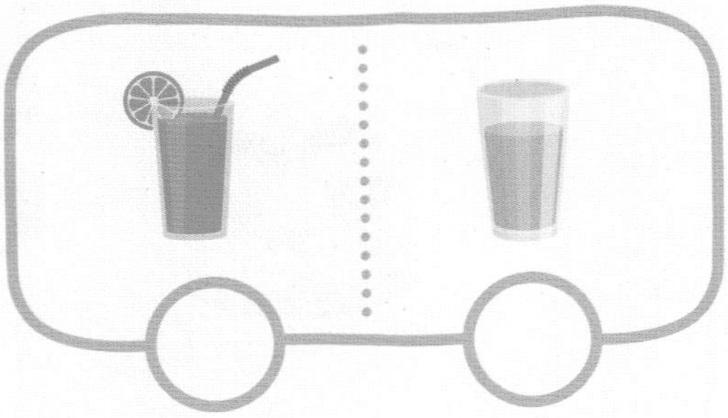

3

4

POPCORN

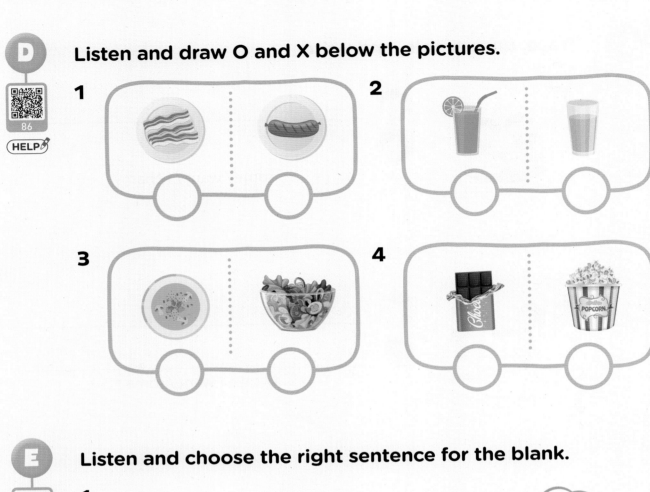

E Listen and choose the right sentence for the blank.

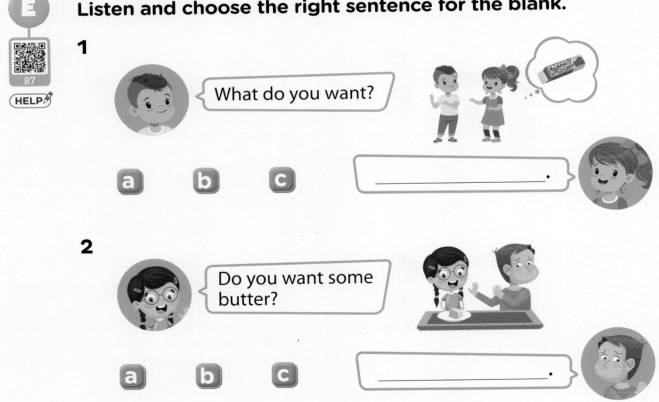

87

HELP

1

What do you want?

a b c

______________________.

2

Do you want some butter?

a b c

______________________.

F Put the dialogue in the correct order.
Then listen to it and practice with a friend.

88
HELP

Wacky: What do you want?

Jack: Do you want some ice cream, too? ☐

Amy: No. I don't want any ice cream. ☐

Jack: I want some ice cream. ☐

Amy: I just want some water.
Do you want some water, too?

Jack: No. I don't want any water.

YOUR TURN! Choose one item and complete the sentences.

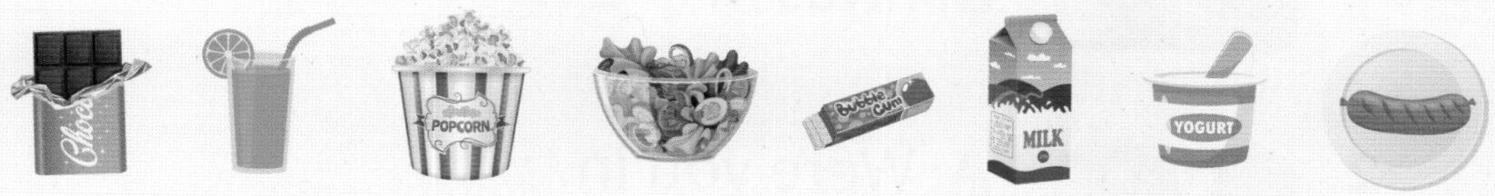
POPCORN
MILK
YOGURT

I want some ______________________________.

I don't want any ______________________________.

UNIT 05

I was in the bedroom.

A Look and write. Use the hints from the cue box.

HELP

1 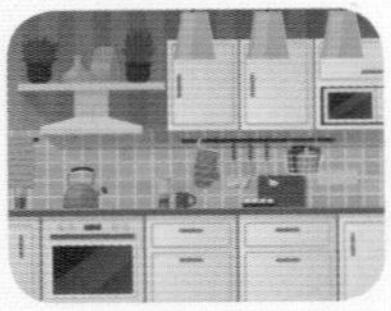

2 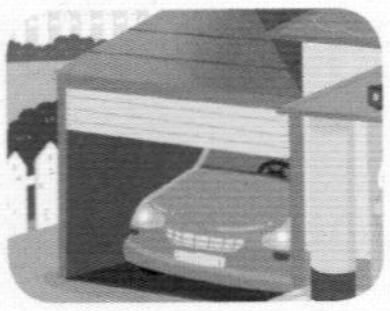

3 

4 

5 

6 

Cue Box

backyard	house	kitchen
garden	bathroom	garage

B Were you there? Look and complete the sentences.

HELP

1 

A: Where were you?

B: I was in the s__________ r__________.

2 

A: Were you in the b__________?

B: Yes. I was in the b__________.

3 

A: Were you in the living room?

B: No. I wasn't in the l__________ r__________.

C Trace, unscramble, and write.

HELP

1

Where were you?

in / I / the dining room / was /.

2

Were you in the living room?

Yes.

the living room / in / I / was /.

3

Where were you?

was / in / I / the kitchen /.

4

Were you in the garage?

No.

I / in / the garage / wasn't /.

in / the garden / was / I /.

D Where were you? Listen and number.

89

HELP

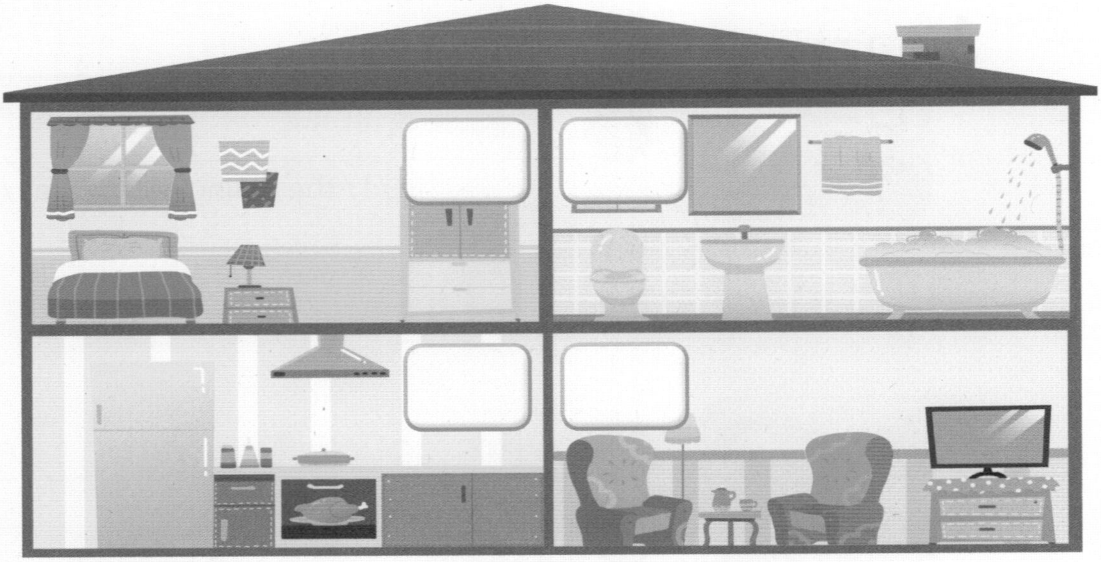

E Listen and choose the right sentence for the blank.

90

HELP

1

Where were you all day?

______________________.

a b c

2

Were you in the garage?

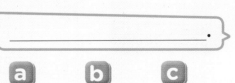

______________________.

a b c

F

91

HELP

Put the dialogue in the correct order.
Then listen to it and practice with a friend.

Mom: Were you in the living room, Jack? ☐

Mom: Where was Lily this morning? ☐

Jack: No. I wasn't in the living room. ☐

Wacky: I don't know. Where was she?

Jack: I remember! She was in the living room!

YOUR TURN! Where were you? Check in the house and complete the sentence.

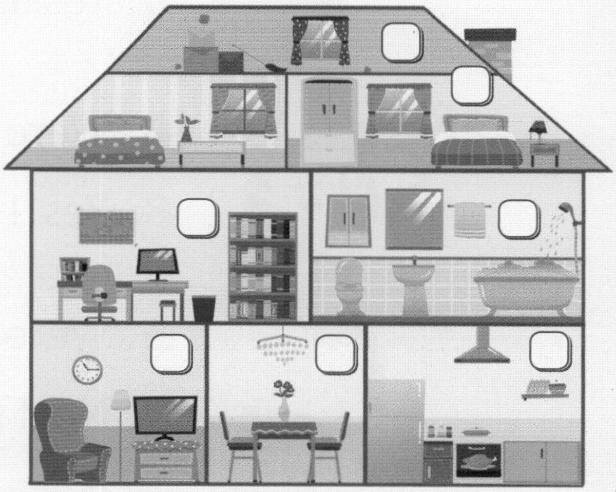

A: Where were you all day?

B: I was in ______________________

______________________.

UNIT 06

I was nervous.

A Write and find the words.

HELP

1 

4 

2 

5 

3 

6 

s	i	t	z	e	b	t	c	r	q
q	w	z	n	w	c	l	a	w	b
d	y	q	e	t	r	j	l	j	r
c	b	o	r	e	d	s	m	s	a
r	q	r	v	n	z	a	z	e	v
a	m	t	o	k	u	d	r	d	e
q	s	q	u	r	m	p	r	e	r
m	x	m	s	r	s	t	s	a	y
s	q	s	t	a	o	r	g	e	r
t	i	r	e	d	k	e	r	y	t

B Look and complete the sentences.

HELP

1 

A: Were you s____________________?

B: Yes. I was s____________________.

2 

A: Were you a____________________?

B: Yes. I was a____________________.

3 

A: Were you bored?

B: No. I wasn't b____________________.

I was g____________________.

C Trace, unscramble, and write.

HELP

1

Were you curious?

Yes. ______________________

I / curious / was / .

2

HAUNTED
HOUSE

Were you glad?

No. ______________________

wasn't / I / glad / .

____

nervous / I / was / .

3

Were you surprised?

Yes. ______________________

was / I / surprised / .

4

Were you upset?

No. ______________________

I / upset / wasn't / .

____

calm / was / I / .

D How did you feel? Listen and number.

92 HELP

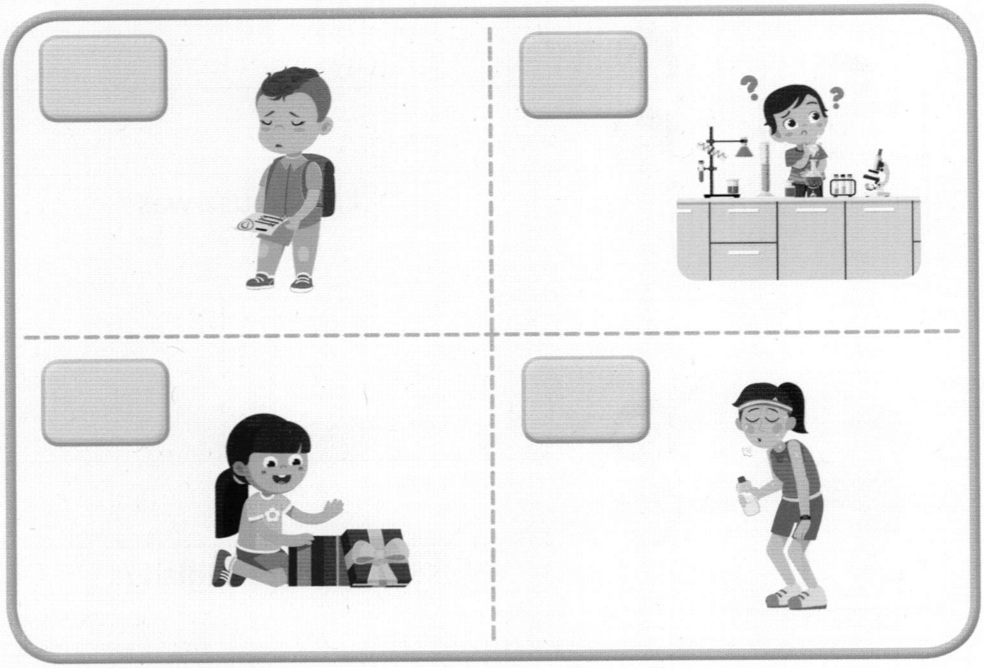

E Listen and choose the right sentence for the blank.

93 HELP

1

Were you upset?

a b c ______________________.

2

Were you nervous?

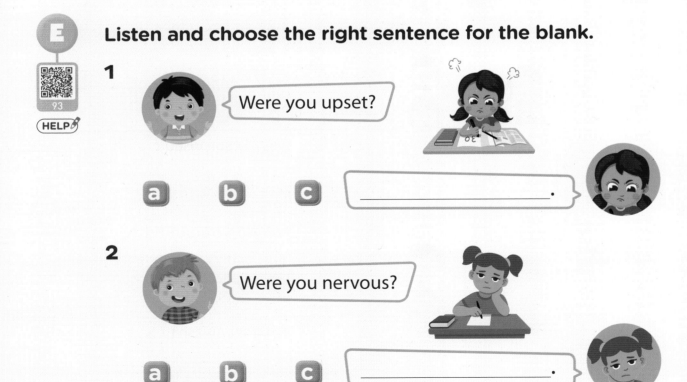

a b c ______________________.

F Put the dialogue in the correct order.
Then listen to it and practice with a friend.

94

HELP

Wacky: Were you nervous?

Jack: Yes. I was so nervous. ☐

Wacky: No. I wasn't bored. ☐

Jack: Were you bored? ☐

Wacky: Your mom was so excited!

Mom: Congratulations.
I am so proud of you.

Jack: Thanks.

YOUR TURN! Look and complete the sentences.

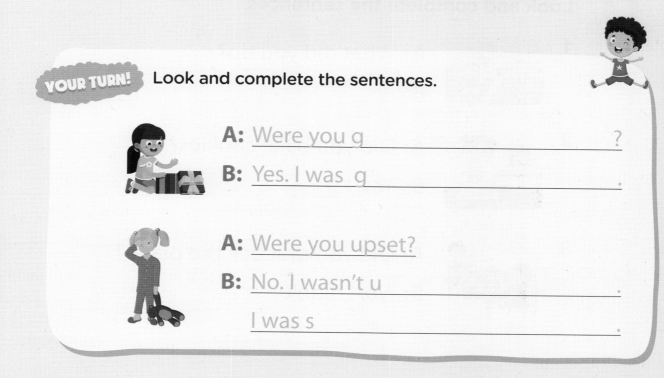

A: Were you g________________?

B: Yes. I was g________________.

A: Were you upset?

B: No. I wasn't u________________.

I was s________________.

UNIT 07 I played football.

A Fill in the blanks below each picture to complete the word.

HELP

1 

___ at ___ ___ ed
TV

2 

p ___ i ___ t ___ d
a picture

3 

___ o ___ ___ ed
dinner

4 

___ t ___ d ___ ed
math

5 

p ___ t ___ ed
a cat

6 

___ a ___ h ___ d
the car

B Look and complete the sentences.

HELP

1 

A: What did you do?

B: I p________________ f________________.

2 

A: Did you bake cookies?

B: Yes. I b________________ c________________.

3 

A: Did you practice the piano?

B: No. I didn't p________________ the p________________.

I p________________ c________________.

C Trace, unscramble, and write.

HELP

1

What did you do?

____

the room / cleaned / I / .

2

Did you walk the dog?

Yes. ____________________

walked / I / the dog / .

3

What did you do?

____

to music / listened / I / .

4

Did you cook dinner?

No. ____________________

cook / didn't / I / dinner / .

____

the dog / I / brushed / .

D What did you do? Listen and number.

95 HELP

E Listen and choose the right sentence for the blank.

96 HELP

1

Did you watch TV?

a b c

____________________.

2

What did you do?

a b c

____________________.

F Put the dialogue in the correct order. Then listen to it and practice with a friend.

97

HELP

Mom: What did you do today?

Jack: I played football and studied math.

Wacky: But we cooked dinner! ☐

Mom: Did you practice the piano? ☐

Jack: No. I didn't practice the piano. Sorry. ☐

Mom: That's okay. You cooked dinner. Thank you.

YOUR TURN! Choose the activities. Write what you did and didn't do in the past.

A: What did you do? Did you ____________________?

B: Yes. I ____________, but I didn't ____________.

UNIT 08 I had fun.

A Unscramble and write the words.

HELP

1 

a s g n

a song

2 

a k d r n

soda

3 

e o r d

a bike

4 

o t o k

a bath

5 

d d i

my homework

6 

a n r

a mile

B Look and complete the sentences.

HELP

1 
Soda
MILK

A: I d__________ soda.

B: I didn't d__________ s__________.

2 

A: I r__________ a b__________.

B: I didn't r__________ a b__________.

3 

A: I a__________ a h__________ __________.

B: I didn't e__________ a h__________ __________.

C Trace, unscramble, and write.

HELP

1 

What did you do?

I played with my friend.

____

had / fun / I / .

2 

What did you do?

____

I / my dog / fed / .

3 

What did you do?

____

a kite / I / flew / .

4 

Did you go to a baseball game?

No.

didn't / to a baseball game / I / go /.

____

rode / I / a bike / .

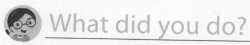

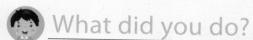

D What did you do? Listen and number.

98

HELP

SODA

E Listen and choose the right sentence for the blank.

99

HELP

1

What did you do?

a b c

________________.

2

What did you do?

a b c

________________.

F

100

HELP

Put the dialogue in the correct order.
Then listen to it and practice with a friend.

Jack: I went to a baseball game with Wacky. ☐

Jack: Yes. I had fun! I saw famous players! ☐

Mom: Did you have fun? ☐

Wacky: No. I didn't have fun.

Mom: What did you eat?

Jack: I ate a hot dog. Mmm, so good!

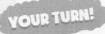

YOUR TURN! **Choose the activities. Write and talk about what you did last weekend with your friends.**

A: What did you do last weekend?

B: I ______________________, but I didn't ______________________.

WORKBOOK GUIDE

HELP

- Try to do the workbook activities on your own as much as possible.
- If you need additional help or want to hear the answers, scan the appropriate QR code below using your phone.
- You will be able to listen to the teacher's explanation immediately!

UNIT 01

A B C D E F

UNIT 02

A B C D E F

UNIT 03

A B C D E F

UNIT 04

A B C D E F

UNIT 05

A B C D E F

UNIT 06

A B C D E F

UNIT 07

A B C D E F

UNIT 08

A B C D E F

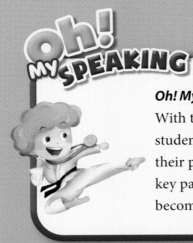

Oh! My Speaking is a six-level speaking series designed for young learners. With task-based activities and vivid illustrations, *Oh! My Speaking* allows students to build up their confidence in speaking and to communicate with their peers in fun and interesting ways. By focusing on basic key words and key patterns with *Oh! My Speaking*, students set out on the journey toward becoming strong speakers of English.

Oh! My Speaking Series

Oh! My SPEAKING 1
Oh! My SPEAKING 2
Oh! My SPEAKING 3
Oh! My SPEAKING 4
Oh! My SPEAKING 5
Oh! My SPEAKING 6

세이펜과 함께 배우는 Oh! My Speaking

〈Oh! My Speaking〉은 세이펜이 적용된 도서입니다. 세이펜을 가져다 대면 원어민의 생생한 영어 발음과 억양을 듣고 영어 말하기 연습을 할 수 있습니다.
*번역 기능 | 세이펜으로 책을 찍어서 원어민 음성을 들은 후, Ⓣ 버튼을 짧게 누르면 우리말 해석 음원을 들을 수 있습니다.

세이펜을 대면 유닛명을 들을 수 있습니다. Ⓣ기능 지원

QR코드에 세이펜을 대면 해당 MP3파일이 재생됩니다.

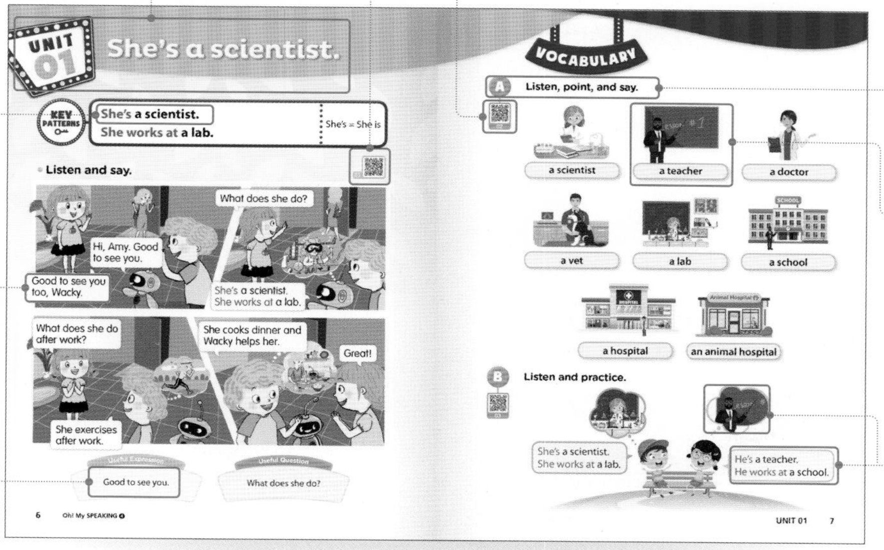

UNIT 01
She's a scientist.
KEY PATTERNS
She's a scientist.
She works at a lab.
She's = She is
Listen and say.
What does she do?
Hi, Amy. Good to see you.
Good to see you too, Wacky.
She's a scientist. She works at a lab.
What does she do after work?
She cooks dinner and Wacky helps her.
Great!
She exercises after work.
Good to see you.
What does she do?
VOCABULARY
Listen, point, and say.
a scientist
a teacher
a doctor
a vet
a lab
a school
a hospital
an animal hospital
Listen and practice.
She's a scientist. She works at a lab.
He's a teacher. He works at a school.
6 Oh! My SPEAKING
UNIT 01 7

세이펜을 대면 Activity의 지시문을 들을 수 있습니다. Ⓣ기능 지원

그림이나 영어 단어에 세이펜을 대면 원어민의 발음을 들을 수 있습니다. Ⓣ기능 지원

그림이나 말풍선에 세이펜을 대면 해당 문장을 들을 수 있습니다. Ⓣ기능 지원

영어 문장에 세이펜을 대면 원어민의 정확한 발음과 억양을 들을 수 있습니다. Ⓣ기능 지원

번호에 세이펜을 대면 해당 그림에 대한 Key Pattern 대화가 재생되며, 그림이나 영어 단어에 세이펜을 대면 해당 영어 단어를 들을 수 있습니다. Ⓣ기능 지원

영어 문장이나 단어에 세이펜을 대면 원어민의 정확한 발음과 억양을 들을 수 있습니다. Ⓣ기능 지원

그림에 세이펜을 대면 해당 그림에 대한 Key Pattern 대화를 들을 수 있습니다. Ⓣ기능 지원

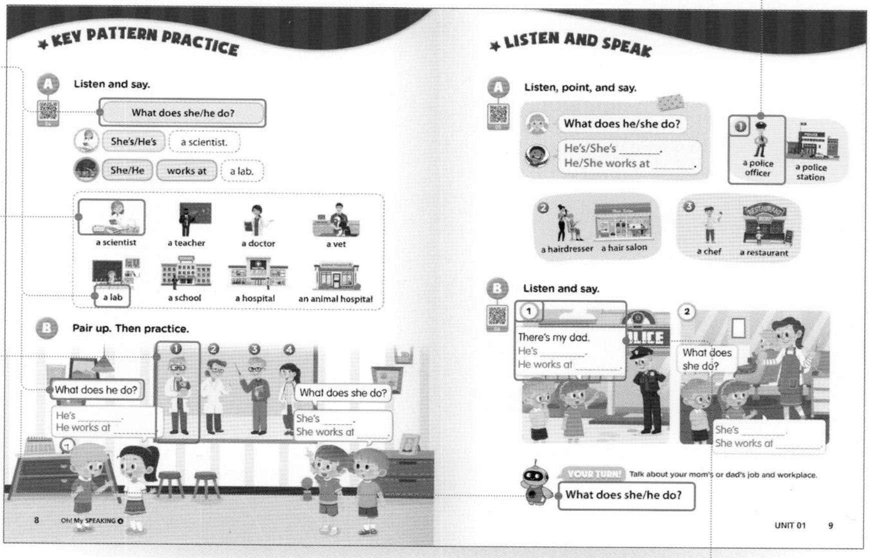

KEY PATTERN PRACTICE
Listen and say.
What does she/he do?
She's/He's
a scientist.
She/He
works at
a lab.
a scientist
a teacher
a doctor
a vet
a lab
a school
a hospital
an animal hospital
Pair up. Then practice.
What does he do?
What does she do?
LISTEN AND SPEAK
Listen, point, and say.
What does he/she do?
He's/She's
He/She works at
a police officer
a police station
a hairdresser
a hair salon
a chef
a restaurant
Listen and say.
There's my dad.
What does she do?
YOUR TURN! Talk about your mom's or dad's job and workplace.
What does she/he do?
8 Oh! My SPEAKING
UNIT 01 9

문제 번호에 세이펜을 대면 해당 문제의 음원이 재생되며, 말풍선에 세이펜을 대면 해당 문장 또는 정답 영어 문장을 들을 수 있습니다. Ⓣ기능 지원

문제 번호나 그림에 세이펜을 대면 해당 문제의 음원이 재생됩니다. Ⓣ기능 지원

문제 번호에 세이펜을 대면 해당 문제의 음원이 재생됩니다.

세이펜을 대면 각 선택지를 들을 수 있습니다. Ⓣ기능 지원

세이펜을 대면 활동 방법을 들을 수 있습니다. 말풍선에 세이펜을 대면 해당 영어 문장을 들을 수 있습니다. Ⓣ기능 지원

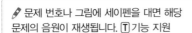

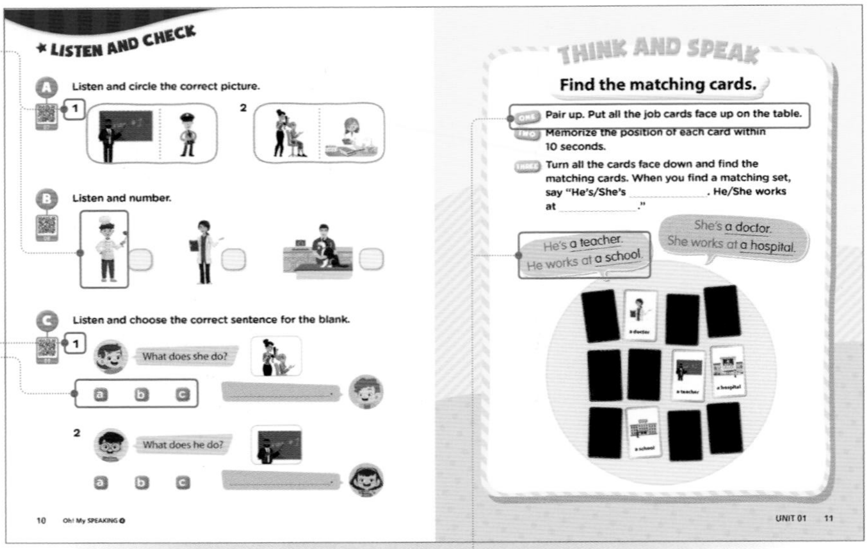

LISTEN AND CHECK
A Listen and circle the correct picture.
B Listen and number.
C Listen and choose the correct sentence for the blank.
What does she do?
What does he do?
THINK AND SPEAK
Find the matching cards.
Pair up. Put all the job cards face up on the table.
Memorize the position of each card within 10 seconds.
Turn all the cards face down and find the matching cards. When you find a matching set, say "He's/She's ______. He/She works at ______."
He's a teacher. He works at a school.
She's a doctor. She works at a hospital.
10 Oh! My SPEAKING
UNIT 01 11

그림이나 영어 단어에 세이펜을 대면 원어민의 발음을 들을 수 있습니다. Ⓣ기능 지원

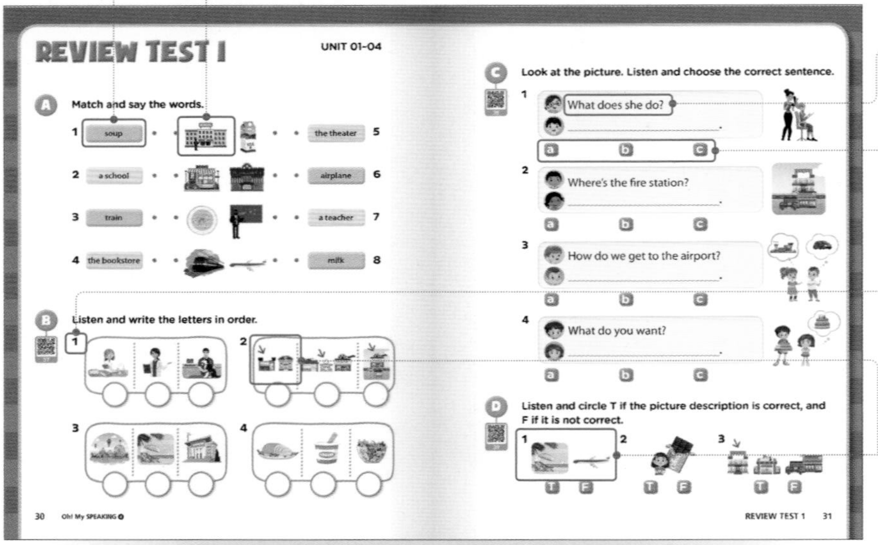

REVIEW TEST 1
UNIT 01-04
A Match and say the words.
soup
a school
train
the bookstore
the theater
airplane
a teacher
milk
B Listen and write the letters in order.
C Look at the picture. Listen and choose the correct sentence.
What does she do?
Where's the fire station?
How do we get to the airport?
What do you want?
D Listen and circle T if the picture description is correct, and F if it is not correct.
30 Oh! My SPEAKING
REVIEW TEST 1 31

세이펜을 대면 해당 문장을 들을 수 있습니다. Ⓣ기능 지원

세이펜을 대면 각 선택지를 들을 수 있습니다. Ⓣ기능 지원

문제 번호에 세이펜을 대면 해당 문제의 음원이 재생됩니다.

그림에 세이펜을 대면 해당 문제를 들을 수 있습니다. Ⓣ기능 지원

세이펜을 대면 선생님의 Workbook Guide를 들을 수 있습니다. HELP

그림 또는 빈칸에 세이펜을 대면 정답 영어 단어를 들을 수 있습니다. Ⓣ기능 지원

그림에 세이펜을 대면 전체 대화를 들을 수 있습니다. Ⓣ기능 지원

세이펜을 대면 정답 또는 해당 문장을 들을 수 있습니다. Ⓣ기능 지원

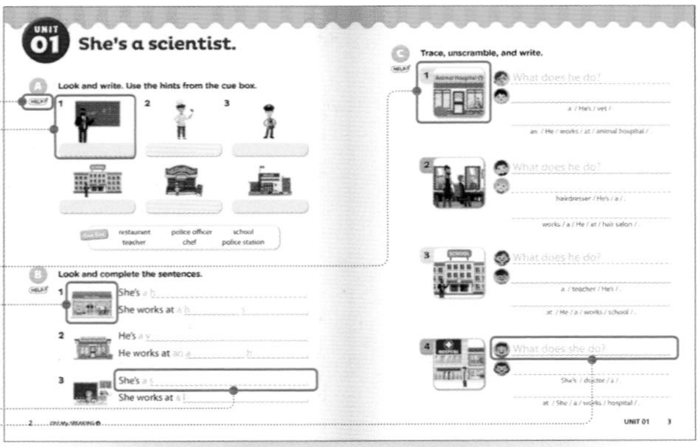

UNIT 01 She's a scientist.
A Look and write. Use the hints from the cue box.
B Look and complete the sentences.
C Trace, unscramble, and write.